Experimental Cooking

Margaret A Brown
Birmingham College of Food and Domestic Arts

Allan G Cameron
Birmingham College of Food and Domestic Arts

Edward Arnold

First published 1977
by Edward Arnold (Publishers) Ltd
25 Hill Street, London W1X 8LL

ISBN: 0 7131 0058 3

Printed in Great Britain by Unwin Brothers Ltd
The Gresham Press, Old Woking

Contents

Preface

This book has been written to bridge the gap between Food Science books on the one hand and Cookery books on the other. It aims at bringing together science and cooking by applying a scientific approach to cookery. The thirty experimental units in the book cover all the main types of food including convenience foods; each unit applies the methods of science to cooking so that the student gains a real *understanding* of what happens to food when it is cooked.

Experimental Cooking has been designed as a series of flexible units that can be carried out in any order; it is therefore adaptable to different teaching programmes. It can also be used at different levels. For example, a selection of the experiments could be used in schools by Home Economics students doing GCE 'O' level and CSE work, while a more comprehensive selection could be attempted by 'A' level students. In Colleges of Further Education students undertaking OND or HND Courses in Catering Subjects or Courses in Home Economics would profit from carrying out the complete course.

Although cooking has traditionally been a subject for girls, *Experimental Cooking,* because it adopts a scientific approach, should appeal equally to girls and boys. A selection of the units would form a suitable experimental basis for an applied science programme in schools in, for example, a Nuffield Course or an integrated course of science and home economics in a RSLA programme. The experiments can usually be undertaken either in a laboratory or a kitchen area.

The authors make no great claim to originality but the experiments are designed to be as 'student proof' as possible and they have all been tried and tested by a variety of students. If users of the book discover any ambiguities, misleading instructions or errors the authors would be glad to know of them.

Introduction

Cooking and science

Cooking is an art. Cooking methods have developed over centuries as man has learnt ways of improving food. He has learnt, for example, how to improve the flavour of food by cooking it. He has learnt the art of combining flavours in cooking (pineapple with cooked ham, sweet and sour pork) and of cooking food with herbs and spices to increase its palatability. The number of books on cooking is enormous — and this is only possible because the art of cooking is a personal one so that each book is different and reflects the differing experience and personalities of the authors.

Cooking is not a science! Cooking involves personal flair and inventiveness; it aims at creating something that appeals to the senses of sight, taste and smell. Science aims at finding out by experimenting; it measures properties and changes; it aims at being clinical and objective and at answering questions of How? and Why? Cooking and Science are so different that they are each carried out in completely different areas; could anybody mistake a kitchen for a laboratory?

In schools cooking is cooking and science is science (even when it is food science) and they are separate worlds. Food science sounds as if it ought to have some relationship with cooking but usually it does not — it is more science than food and often involves chemical tests carried out on food. Such tests may tell us whether starch is present, whether salt has been added and the nature of the sugar present but such tests seem a far cry from the realities of the kitchen.

In this book we are not concerned with cookery as an art nor with science as a series of tests that can be applied to food. What we are concerned with is the bringing together of cooking and science by applying a scientific approach to cooking. In other words we are going to apply the methods of science to cooking so that we can answer the How? and Why? questions about cooking. In this way we hope to gain an understanding of cooking as well as being able to do it.

Science and cooking

When we use the term a *scientific approach* we mean planning and controlling carefully what we do so that we can find out the particular information we need. The proper design of experiments involves control of the many factors that may vary and this extremely important aspect is discussed in more detail later.

Cooking — an art (left) or a science (right)?

In the experiments that follow a scientific approach has been applied to methods of cooking and it will be found that such experiments can be carried out in either kitchens or laboratories with some modifications. If a laboratory is used some kitchen utensils and some kitchen equipment (such as cookers with ovens) will be required. If a kitchen is used some laboratory equipment (such as normal glass-ware — and distillation apparatus for unit 18 and titration equipment for units 2 and 17) and chemicals will need to be borrowed from the Science department. The fact that experimental cookery can be carried out in either kitchen or laboratory serves to emphasise that the experiments which follow aim to bring together the normally separate areas of science and cooking.

Format of the experiments

Each of the units is intended to be complete in itself and with few exceptions one unit occupies two facing pages so that the whole unit is visible at a glance. Most units are designed round a particular commodity, and this emphasises that our prime concern is with cooking. The format adopted allows maximum flexibility as the units can be carried out in any order.

1 Aims

In cooking it is not helpful to follow a recipe slavishly without any thought of what you are trying to achieve. Similarly in these experiments it is not helpful simply to carry out the instructions without any thought of the aims of the experiment. One reason why students often consider experiments a 'waste of time' is that they don't understand the reasons for what they are doing; if the aims are kept in mind throughout it is hoped that this danger will be avoided.

2 Introduction

Each unit includes a brief explanation of the theory upon which the experimental work is based. This is intended to improve understanding of the practical work but as only an outline can be given, books of reference are included at the end of the book for those requiring a fuller treatment of the subject.

3 Required

This section itemises all the equipment and materials (both foods and chemicals) required.

a *Chemicals* Most of the chemicals required are common ones that will be readily available in the science laboratory. A very few special chemicals are required (e.g. Fehlings solutions I and II and Millon's reagent in unit 5) and if these are not kept by the laboratory they can be ordered from the suppliers mentioned in appendix 1.

b *Foodstuffs* The quantities of food given are sufficient for one person to carry out all the experiments in a unit. In the interests of economy of time and materials it is expected that the experiments in a unit will be divided between members of a class, so that the complete unit can be carried out in one practical session of 2 - 3 hours.

4 Method

The method is given in sufficient detail to enable anyone without special knowledge to carry out the experiments successfully.

5 Questions

Questions are an integral part of the text. Most of them relate directly to observations that should be made during an experiment though some — particularly those at the end of units — are designed to draw out more general points.

6 Follow up

The amount that can be described in each unit is limited and the object of the follow up sections is to suggest things to do or find out that will extend the interest and range covered by the unit.

A scientific approach

In unit 15.1 there is a recipe for making a Victoria Sandwich cake. The procedure is simple and clearly laid out; but if 20 people follow this recipe it will be surprising if any 2 cakes are exactly the same.

The reason for these differences is that there are so many variables involved such as different raw materials, equipment, handling techniques or cooking conditions, all of which affect the result. For example, it is unlikely that any two ovens will have exactly the same performance or even that two cakes cooked in the same oven will be identical as they can not be situated in exactly the same position in the oven.

It is hard to standardise even such a simple operation as creaming.

To make a standard cake, all conditions and operations would have to be standardised *precisely* including raw materials, amounts, temperatures and even types of equipment. It is obviously difficult to turn cooking into science!

In making a scientific approach to something involving as many variables as cooking it is necessary to control the variables. Ideally all variables are controlled except one. It is then possible to observe and evaluate the effect of this one variable. To take a simple example; consider the boiling of an egg. Provided that standard eggs are used it is possible to boil eggs at the same temperature (100^0C) for different lengths of time and, after cooling, note the effect of different cooking times on quality. The only variable involved is time. In unit 8.1

and that eggs should be taken from a bulk supply.

Meat is an example of a raw material where it is difficult to obtain uniform quality, but where a piece is cut into smaller samples for different treatments it is important that the quality should be fairly uniform. For instance, if the lean meat in unit 11.1 is not uniform, it is difficult to compare effectively the tenderised samples with the control.

Controlling the number of variables in cooking is not often as easy as when boiling eggs where only cooking time needs to be controlled. Would you expect cooking time to vary for the different eggs shown?

both the times and temperatures of cooking are varied in order to find the best combination for a high quality egg. Unless the same *size* of egg is used throughout a new variable will be introduced and it will be impossible to interpret the results.

The use of controls
Experiment 8.2 describes a scientific approach to poaching eggs. Firstly the method of poaching is standardised (temperature and time are both fixed). Then, in order to find out how the addition of various substances to the cooking water affects the quality, a *control* is used against which the quality of the other eggs is judged.

Similarly in unit 9, the basic recipe for producing a standard egg custard is used as a control, and the functions of various ingredients are studied by altering the different factors in turn and comparing the result with the control.

In the experiments that follow controls are often used to act as a standard from which variations can be detected.

Ingredients
In attempting a scientific approach to cooking, the quality and uniformity of ingredients used needs to be standardised. For example, in unit 15.2, batches of biscuits are made using different flours. As flour is the only variable the other ingredients should be of the same quality in every batch. This means that the sugar and margarine should be from the same packet

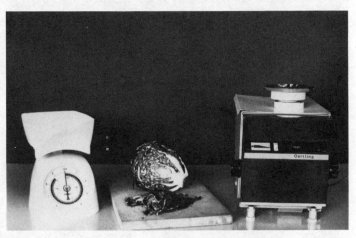

Weighings should always be made on scales which are appropriate to the accuracy required. A single pan balance (right) is accurate: kitchen scales (left) are not. Which balance would be more suitable for weighing approximately 100g of red cabbage?

Accuracy
This is a vexed subject with students who, when quoting a weight, think it more impressive to quote the result as 100.000g rather than 100g! If an accurate balance has been used (see photo) it may of course be quite appropriate to quote 3 places of decimals but if a very rough balance, such as kitchen scales, has been used it is more realistic to give the result as 100g or even approx. 100g.

In the experiments that follow it is necessary that some weighings are done as accurately as possible whereas others can be quite approximate. It is important for students to realise this, and to select a balance appropriate to the accuracy required. For example, in experiment 7.1 the weights of different sizes of egg are to be compared and weighings should be as accurate as possible. On the other hand in experiment 18.2 samples of vegetables are to be cooked for different lengths of time and the method specifies approximately 400g samples. Here the exact weight is not important as only flavour, texture and colour are being assessed and the weighings can be done very roughly.

In unit 10.1, where samples of meat are weighed before and after cooking, it is difficult to avoid weighing meat juices as well, and further inaccuracies are introduced if the meat is weighed hot. Also, the errors involved in calculating the percentage weight loss are such that it is pointless to quote answers other than as whole numbers. If the method itself is inaccurate, it is pointless trying to weigh accurately or to quote answers which imply high accuracy.

7

Volume

Measurements of volume are made more frequently than any other in the experiments that follow. The accuracy of volume measurements using different types of measuring equipment is just as variable as weight measurements using different types of balance. Household measuring devices, such as teaspoons, cups and graduated jugs are not accurate because they have a large surface area. For example, in measuring a cupful of flour it is impossible to know precisely when the cup is 'full'. Such domestic equipment should only be used therefore when approximate amounts are required.

Laboratory equipment for measuring volume, of increasing accuracy from left to right: beaker, measuring cylinder, burette and pipette (all of 50 cm³ capacity).

Scientific equipment for measuring volume (see photo) varies from very approximate (e.g. a beaker) to very accurate (e.g. a pipette). When students select a piece of equipment to measure a volume they should think whether the measurement needs to be accurate or not. They should also select equipment of the appropriate size; for example, if 1cm³ of a liquid is to be measured it would be more appropriate to use a 1cm³ pipette than a 100 cm³ measuring cylinder.

In unit 11.2 meat is to be cooked in approximately 100 cm³ water. This volume of water could conveniently be measured in a 100 cm³ measuring cylinder or even in a 100 cm³ beaker. When 5 cm³ vinegar is added it would not be appropriate to use a 100 cm³ measuring cylinder; but it would be convenient and accurate enough to use a 10 cm³ measuring cylinder.

In unit 17 the vitamin C content of fruit and vegetables is to be measured, and the experiment must be carried out as accurately as possible. Note that here scientific equipment of good accuracy — i.e. burettes and pipettes of sizes appropriate to the volumes being measured — is used.

In unit 18.2 vegetables are to be cooked in 500 cm³ water. Read the instructions, decide what level of accuracy is required and select an appropriate measuring device.

In unit 2.1 (b) strengths of different vinegars are to be compared. Why do you think that this experiment is carried out using pipettes and burettes as measuring devices?

Note. When measuring a volume in a burette obtain consistent readings by always putting a piece of paper behind the burette and reading the bottom of the meniscus with your eye at the same level as the meniscus.

Planning experimental work

1 Read through the complete unit before you start and make sure you appreciate the aims and underlying theory.
2 Collect together the materials and equipment you will require.
3 Plan the order of what you are going to do, and work systematically and tidily. Wash up dirty equipment as you go along.
4 As you are handling food, work according to rules of good hygiene. Ensure cleanliness of equipment, surfaces and materials. Wear clean protective clothing to guard you from spills and food from contamination. (Headgear that encloses the hair is important). Hands and nails should be kept clean. Avoid contamination of food by chemicals.

Recording experimental work

1 Note all observations at the time they are made in a durable notebook or file. Accuracy and completeness of observations are more important than beauty in writing up the experiment!
2 Note any changes made in the prescribed method, and write down answers to all the questions asked.
3 Some of the experiments involve *objective* assessment i.e. results are based on measurement made using equipment rather than relying on human judgement. Such objective measurements include weight, volume and temperature when measured by scientific equipment. For example, if the temperature of warm water is measured with a thermometer the result is objective, if it is judged with a finger it is not.
Example. In unit 17 the vitamin C content of fruit and vegetables is to be determined. The method involves

objective measurements (apart from a judgement of colour) and the result is therefore a definite measured quantity rather than a human judgement.

4 Many of the experiments involve *subjective* assessment, i.e. they depend upon human judgement of such ill defined qualities as flavour, texture and colour. It is important to appreciate that such judgements reflect personal preferences and are therefore more liable to human error and inconsistency than objective methods.

In assessing food objective measurements may not be possible and in any case in evaluating such factors as flavour or texture a subjective assessment may be more relevant because we are concerned with personal reaction. For example, it is possible to measure factors relating to the texture of meat with instruments but it may be more useful for texture or 'chewability' to be judged by chewing the meat. If the texture of meat is unpleasantly tough no instrument can detect this as fast or as efficiently as a human being!

In attempting to record subjective factors such as flavour as objectively as possible, a scientific approach is necessary. For example, in unit 22.1 textured and spun proteins are compared with meat and to make this comparison a hedonic scale is used i.e. a scale that indicates the extent of like or dislike for a food. The use of other scales in flavour assessment is discussed in unit 29.

5 Once an experiment has been carried out and the observations recorded, then it is necessary to interpret the data and draw conclusions. The conclusions reached are one of the most important aspects of recording an experiment and if conclusions are not drawn the whole value of the experiment may be lost. For example, in unit 18.2 methods of cooking vegetables are investigated and at the end of the experiment recommendations of how best to cook different vegetables are asked for. If this is not done, or not done correctly, little practical value will be gained from the experimental work carried out.

1 Water—and its importance in cooking

Aims

1 To introduce the student to some basic principles and techniques.
2 To investigate whether the type of water used in cooking has any effect on the end product.

Introduction

Of all the materials used in cooking, water is the commonest — and the cheapest. It is so common that perhaps we fail to notice what a remarkable substance it is. Its particular properties make it uniquely suited for the endless purposes for which it is used — including cooking.

Pure water is a colourless, odourless and tasteless liquid that freezes at $0°C$ and boils at $100°C$. The boiling point of water increases however when substances are dissolved in it, and the amount of the increase depends on the amount dissolved. Thus water containing dissolved mineral salts has a boiling point above $100°C$.

Water is said to be *hard* when it does not lather easily with soap. Hardness is due to the presence of certain mineral salts — such as the sulphates and bicarbonates of calcium and magnesium — dissolved in the water. Water is said to be *permanently* hard when the hardness is due to salts such as calcium or magnesium sulphate which do not break down on heating; it is said to be *temporarily* hard when the hardness is due to salts such as calcium bicarbonate that break down on heating.

Water with a pH above 7 (see next experiment) is said to be alkaline, whereas vegetables have a pH below 7 and are said to be acid. If vegetables are cooked in water that is alkaline, colour and texture may be affected. For example, although the colour of green vegetables remains bright, the colour of red vegetables turns purple, and the colour of white vegetables turns yellow. Also, the texture of vegetables becomes soft and mushy.

Required

Equipment
$0-110°C$ thermometer
pans
bunsen burners
tripods
gauzes (or gas rings)
1000 cm^3 and 100 cm^3 beakers (cups)
sharp knives
pH paper (Universal pH 1-14)

Materials:
tea (preferably tea bags)
instant coffee
orange squash
milk
sugar
potatoes
onions
carrots
cabbage (green and red)
(about 250g of each vegetable)
Types of water — distilled, tap, local soft and hard (identified by area name only), laboratory samples of permanently hard water containing calcium or magnesium sulphate, and temporary hard water containing calcium bicarbonate.

How is the quality of tea affected by whether the water is hard or soft (experiment d)?

Salts that cause hardness in water are responsible not only for the effects studied in this unit but also for the formation of stalactites. Try to find out how stalactites are formed.

Method

a *Taste of water.* Taste each sample of water and try to describe any differences you observe.

b *Taste of orange squash.* Repeat **a** but add an equal volume of orange squash to each sample. Does this make it easier or harder to describe any differences?

c *Boiling points.* Boil an equal volume of each sample of water in a large beaker and observe any differences. Boil vigorously for several minutes and measure the boiling point of each sample (using the same thermometer); also observe any changes in the appearance of the samples.

d *Effect of water on the quality of tea.* Using some of the boiling water from **c** make up a cup of tea from each sample of water by adding the same amount of boiling water to the same amount of dry tea each time. Stir well.
If using tea bags leave each in the water for the same time. Note any differences in the colour, taste and smell of the black tea. Add an equal amount of milk to each, and sugar if liked, and again observe the colour, taste and smell. Let the tea stand for 10 minutes and note any colour changes and also if any residue is left in the cup or beaker.

e *Effect of water on the quality of coffee.* Repeat **d** but use instant coffee, first black and then with addition of cold milk.
Note. **d** and **e** are useful exercises in the difficult job of controlling all the variables except the one in question.

f *Effect of water on the quality of boiled onions.* Peel and roughly chop some onions and divide into the correct number of equal samples. Boil each sample of onions in the different waters for exactly 20 minutes and record the differences in colour and texture.

g *Effect of water on the quality of boiled cabbage and carrots.* Repeat **f** with samples of shredded green cabbage, shredded red cabbage and sliced carrots.

h *pH.* Record the pH of each water using pH indicator paper. (See next experiment for discussion of pH).

Questions

What are the differences in the nature of distilled water, temporary hard water and permanently hard water?
Why do some tea companies produce different brands of tea for use in soft and hard water areas?
What can you say about the nature of your school's tap water and of the local area water samples supplied to you?
How do you explain the fact that the boiling point of different types of water may vary?
What are the disadvantages of using hard water for cooking vegetables?
Why might vinegar be added to red cabbage and sodium bicarbonate to green cabbage when they are boiled?

Follow up

Find out the nature of the changes that occur in cabbage when it is boiled (see unit 16).

2 pH–and its importance in cooking

Aims

1 To show that the concept of acids and bases is relevant to cooking.
2 To introduce the student to quantitative techniques (using pipettes and burettes).

Introduction

Acids are easy to recognise; they have a sour taste, they alter the colour of substances known as indicators (e.g. they turn blue litmus paper red) and they attack many metals. Alkalis (or bases as they are also called) are equally easy to recognise; they often have a soapy feel and strong alkalis have a caustic or burning action on the skin; they change the colour of indicators (e.g. they turn red litmus blue).

Acids react with alkalis to form salts:
Acid + Base → Salt + Water.
This reaction may be used to measure the acid strength of a food such as vinegar. Vinegar contains *acetic acid* and if a base is added to vinegar, the acid is converted to a salt. When all the acid has been used up it is said to have been *neutralized* by the base. The neutral point is detected by the colour change in an indicator; it is the point at which the acidity disappears and is known as the *end point* of a *titration*. If the alkali used is of a known strength the amount required to neutralize the acetic acid is a measure of the amount of acid present (see calculation in 1(b)).

It is useful to be able to compare the acidity of different substances using a simple scale, and the *pH scale* is a convenient means of doing this. pH is defined as $- \log_{10}$ (hydrogen ion) concentration but if this means nothing to you, it is enough to appreciate that the pH scale is a 14 point scale with a centre point of pH7 representing neutrality (pure water). Starting at pH7 (see scale below) decreasing pH indicates increasing acidity, whereas increasing pH (i.e. above 7) indicates increasing basicity.

A *buffer solution* is a solution of known and constant pH. It has the advantage that its pH remains constant when small amounts of acid or alkali are added to it.

pH and its control are very important in cooking as will become apparent not only in this experiment but also in those that follow.

Required

Equipment:
dropping pipettes
10 cm³ pipettes
50 cm³ burettes
50 cm³ measuring cylinders
250 cm³ conical flasks
burette stands
pans
knives
test tubes

Materials:
standard solution of sodium hydroxide (16 g sodium hydroxide in 250 cm³ water)
dilute (approx. 2N) hydrochloric acid
sodium bicarbonate
phenolphthalein indicator
buffer tablets or solutions for a range of pH values
(e.g. pH 4.0, 7.0, 9.2)
variety of pH indicator papers
450g carrots
450g onions
225g dried peas
1 red cabbage
selection of different vinegars e.g. malt vinegar, cider vinegar, distilled vinegar (use both expensive and cheap varieties if possible)
Caution. Sodium hydroxide is caustic and burns the skin.

Method

1 Measuring the acidity of acid foods

a *Colour of indicator in acid and alkali.* Put a little hydrochloric acid in a test tube and add a drop of indicator with a dropping pipette. Slowly add sodium hydroxide from a dropping pipette until the colour changes (indicating excess alkali). Note the colour of the indicator in acid and alkali.

b *To compare the strength of different vinegars.* Fill a burette with the sodium hydroxide solution provided (take care!) and adjust the level to the zero mark ensuring that no air

The pH scale showing pH values of selected foods

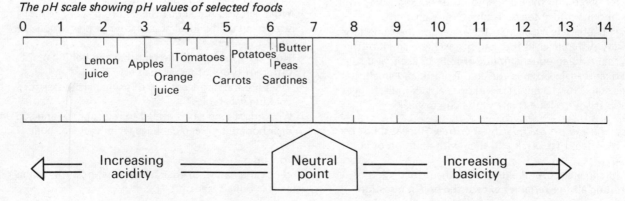

bubbles are present particularly at the bottom of the burette near the tap. Pipette exactly 10 cm³ of one of the vinegars into a clean conical flask and add about 50 cm³ of water and 3 drops of indicator using a dropping pipette. Place the flask under the burette and open the top to allow about 1 cm³ to drip into the vinegar. Shake and if there is no colour change, add a little more sodium hydroxide and shake again. Continue until the vinegar remains a *pale* pink colour. Note the amount of alkali added. Repeat using the same type of vinegar until 2 similar results are obtained (i.e. within 0.1 cm³ of each other).

Carry out the same procedure for the other vinegars.

Calculation

The strength of the sodium hydroxide is such that 1 cm³ is equivalent to 1% acetic acid in the vinegar. Hence knowing the amount of alkali used for each vinegar the percentage acidity of each can be calculated. Compare the strength of the different vinegars. Also compare their tastes.

What is the cost of the different vinegars per 100 cm³? Taking into account their different strengths which is the best value for money?
Which type of vinegar do you consider would be most suitable for (a) preserving white cocktail onions (b) using in the manufacture of a brown sauce such as HP sauce (c) making chutney at home and (d) making French dressing?
The acidity of vinegar can be expressed in 2 different ways. What are they?

c *Comparison of the acidity of fruit juices.* Experiment (**b**) can be repeated using different fruit juices although quantitative results are not possible in the same way (i.e. % of a particular acid present) as most fruit juices contain several different acids. The acidity of different juices can be compared, however, in terms of the amount of sodium hydroxide required to change the colour of the indicator.

2   To show the effect of pH on boiled vegetables
Use made-up buffer solutions, or if buffer tablets are available, add 1 tablet to 100 cm³ water to give the correct pH, e.g. 4.0, 8.0, 9.2. To extend the pH range add dilute hydrochloric acid and sodium bicarbonate until the respective pH's as measured by indicator paper are approximately 2 and 12. For each experiment below cook the vegetables in about 200 cm³ of different pH solutions.

a *Carrots.* Scrape clean and cut into 5 cm long strips, (5 x 1 x 1 cm). Place 6 strips into each solution and boil for 5 minutes. Compare the colour of the different samples; also the texture by flexing the strips or squeezing them between the fingers.

b *Onions.* Peel and chop finely. Divide between the different solutions and boil for 10 minutes. Compare the colour of the onions and also of the cooking liquid for the different samples.

c *Red Cabbage.* Shred finely and divide between the different solutions. Boil for 5 minutes. Compare the colour of the

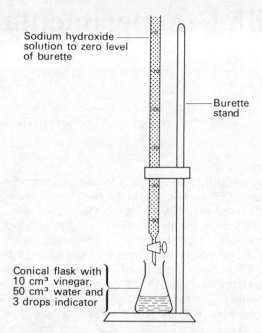

Titration apparatus for measuring the acidity of vinegar

cabbage and of the cooking liquid for the different samples.

d *Dried peas.* Soak over night or for as long as possible in the solutions of different pH. Boil each sample for 15 minutes and compare the colour and texture of the cooked peas.

Questions

Why is pickled red cabbage usually a bright red colour whereas the raw cabbage is often purple?
What could you add to the water when boiling onions to make sure they stay white?
Why is a 'soaking tablet' consisting of sodium bicarbonate provided with some varieties of green peas?

3 Milk I – experimental analysis

Aims
1 To investigate the structure and composition of cow's milk.
2 To examine some of the properties of the nutrients present in milk.

Introduction
The average composition of milk is as follows; 4% fat, 5% milk sugar (lactose), 3.5% protein, 0.5% mineral elements (mainly calcium and phosphate), 87% water, together with small quantities of vitamins, mainly vitamins A and B_2. Although milk is such a watery food it supplies us with a wide variety of nutrients. For example, for a girl aged 9-15 one pint of milk supplies the following proportions of her daily needs; 1/6 energy, 1/3 protein, all the calcium, 1/3-1/4 Vitamin A, 1/5 Vitamin B_1 and 1/2 Vitamin B_2. In terms of food value for money, milk is one of the best buys available. It is not a perfect food, however, because it lacks some nutrients notably iron and vitamins C and D. Milk from the cow does contain some vitamin C, but this is mostly lost during heat treatment (see experiment 4) and through poor storage in warm conditions or in sunlight.

The fat in milk is in the form of very tiny droplets, so small that they can only be seen under the microscope. It is said to be an *emulsion,* and this makes the fat easy to digest. In homogenized milk the fat droplets are dispersed throughout the milk but in pasteurized milk the fat droplets rise to the surface and form a cream layer. This is because the *specific gravity* of fat is less than that of water. Specific gravity is defined as the weight of a material compared with the weight of an equal volume of water.

Milk is an emulsion and although its structure cannot be seen with the naked eye (left) it can be seen with a microscope (right — the light coloured fat droplets are clearly visible).

The main proteins in milk are caseinogen (2.6%), lactalbumin (0.5%) and lactoglobulin (0.2%). Proteins are very sensitive to conditions such as temperature, acidity (pH) and the addition of salts and this has an important bearing on the behaviour of milk. The various proteins in milk differ in their sensitivity however. For example, lactalbumin and lactoglobulin are particularly sensitive to heat so that when milk is heated these proteins *coagulate* i.e. turn solid and form a skin on the surface. On the other hand caseinogen is very sensitive to pH. When milk turns sour (i.e. the pH drops) it *curdles* as the caseinogen is coagulated and forms curds; also caseinogen forms a solid clot in the presence of the enzyme *rennin* contained in rennet, especially at low pH. Enzymes, such as rennin, are themselves proteins and therefore heat sensitive; this explains why they work best at a particular temperature.

Required

Equipment:
microscope and slides
500 cm^3 measuring cylinder
milk lactometer (or specific gravity bottle)
test tubes
test tube rack
1000 cm^3 beaker
250 cm^3 beakers
bunsen burners (or gas rings)
0-110°C thermometer
glass rods
muslin cloth
evaporating dish
cotton wool

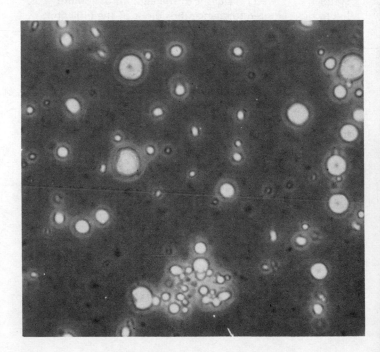

Materials:
3 pints fresh pasteurized milk
ethyl alcohol (or industrial spirit)
approx. 10% solutions of citric acid, lactic acid, acetic acid,
copper sulphate
dilute sodium hydroxide
dilute hydrochloric acid
essence of rennet
lemon juice
vinegar
salt
sodium bicarbonate
sugar
pH indicator papers

Method
1 Milk fat

a *Microscopic examination.* Separate the cream layer from a pint of milk that has been standing for a while. Put a drop of cream on one slide, and a drop of the remaining milk on another and examine under the low power lens of a microscope. Draw diagrams of what you see.

How would you describe and explain the structure of milk and why are the two slides different?

b *Specific gravity.* Pour about 400 cm³ of milk from which the cream has been removed into a 500 cm³ measuring cylinder and measure the specific gravity with a milk lactometer † (range 1.028-1.034). Replace about 100 cm³ of the milk in the cylinder with the cream removed earlier and shake well. Measure the specific gravity of the creamy milk. Return all the milk to the original bottle, shake well, and transfer about 400 cm³ to the cylinder and measure the specific gravity of this whole milk. Dilute the milk with about 20 cm³ of water and measure the specific gravity. Dilute further with another 20 cm³ of water and remeasure the specific gravity.

† *Note.* If a lactometer is not available, the specific gravity can be obtained by comparing the weight of a milk sample with the weight of an equal volume of water.
  From your results explain;
 (i) how the removal of cream affects the specific gravity of milk;
 (ii) how the addition of water affects the specific gravity of milk

This method of analysis is sometimes used in a dairy to check the fat content of milk. How could a farmer cheat the dairy about the standard of his milk?

2 Milk protein

a *Effect of heat.* Warm a sample of milk slowly in a pan or beaker without stirring and note the temperature at which a skin first appears. Continue heating gently, watching what is happening to the skin and the milk under the skin.

Why do you think a skin forms when milk is heated?
Why does milk boil over whereas water would not?

b *Effect of additives.* Pour about 5 cm³ milk into a series of test tubes in a test tube rack. Add about 1 cm³ (or 1g if solid) of the following substances, shake well and leave to stand for a few minutes. Observe any changes in appearance and smell.
Use; alcohol, lemon juice, vinegar, salt, sugar, sodium bicarbonate, hydrochloric acid, sodium hydroxide, citric acid, acetic acid, copper sulphate and rennet.

Which substances cause the biggest change in the milk protein?

c *Action of rennet.* Pour about 5 cm³ milk into 9 labelled test tubes. Put all the test tubes into a 1000 cm³ beaker containing cold water and warm gently. Measure the temperature of the milk in the test tubes (not the water) and remove a tube when the temperature reaches 20°C, another at 30°C, continuing at 10°C intervals until the final tube is removed at 100°C. (Note the temperature on the label of each tube.) Immediately after removing each tube add 2 drops of rennet, shake and leave to cool. Observe what happens in each tube.

What is the best temperature for the action of rennet?

Add about 5 cm³ milk to each of 5 test tubes and warm to about 40°C in a beaker of water. Add one of the following to each tube;
 (i) 5 drops lactic acid,
 (ii) 2 drops lactic acid,
 (iii) 5 drops sodium hydroxide,
 (iv) 2 drops sodium hydroxide,
 (v) no addition
  Measure the pH of each milk with indicator paper, add 2 drops rennet, shake and leave to cool. Observe what happens in each case.

What is the best pH for the action of rennet?

Questions
What is an emulsion? What foods can you think of that are emulsions?
Why does a cream layer form slowly at the top of a bottle of pasteurized milk?
Why is it best to store milk in a cool place out of direct sunlight?
Why is milk not a perfect food? When a baby is weaned off mother's milk and given cow's milk instead, why are supplements of orange juice and cod liver oil often given?

4 Milk II–its use in cooking

Aims
1 To compare various forms of milk in drinks and for cooking.
2 To find out the best way for reconstituting dried milk.
3 To discover the best way of combining acid materials with milk.

Introduction
Although milk is such a valuable food it is also an ideal place for the growth of micro-organisms. In the past many deaths have resulted from milk infected with harmful bacteria, particularly the *tubercle bacillus* which is responsible for causing tuberculosis. This danger has been minimised in Great Britain by ensuring that all cows are *Tuberculin Tested* (free from *tubercle bacillus*) but in addition it is necessary to give milk a heat treatment to make it completely safe and to improve its keeping qualities.

The most common form of heat treatment is *pasteurization* in which milk is heated to at least 72°C for at least 15 seconds and then cooled rapidly. This kills most bacteria without altering taste significantly and causes little loss of nutrients. Pasteurized milk may also be *homogenized* to disperse the fat uniformly to give a finely dispersed stable emulsion. *Sterilized* milk is homogenized and given a severe heat treatment that changes its taste, destroys much of the vitamin B_1 and C and coagulates protein. It will however keep for at least a week and normally much longer. *Ultra-high temperature* (U.H.T.) sterilization of milk involves heating to a high temperature

In a modern dairy automation ensures very high standards of hygiene as is evident in this photograph in which the sequence of washing, filling, capping and crating of bottles of milk can be seen.

(135-150°C) for 1-3 seconds. Such milk resembles pasteurized milk in flavour and food value, but it will keep for several months without refrigeration.

Milk is also available in convenience or preserved form. *Evaporated* milk contains about 70% water and is made by evaporating milk at a low temperature (below 70°C) to prevent coagulation of protein and a 'cooked' flavour. It is sterilized in sealed cans and will keep for long periods. Whole cream milk may be converted into *dried* milk by roller-drying or by spray-drying. The former method produces a product with a cooked flavour and which is only 80% soluble in water. Spray-dried milk tastes more like fresh milk and is almost 100% soluble in water. Unfortunately it is not easily wetted by water and so is not easy to reconstitute. It is sometimes treated to make it easier to reconstitute ('instant' milk powder).

Required
Equipment:
sharp knives
chopping board
pans or large beakers
wooden spoons
teaspoons
test tubes
small beakers or cups (for drinks)
0-110°C thermometer
100 cm³ measuring cylinder
tea pot
gas rings or burners
pH paper (pH 1-14)
Materials:
tea
instant coffee
cocoa or drinking chocolate
custard powder
sugar
essence of rennet (preferably flavoured)
1 pint of each of the following milks — pasteurized, homogenized, skimmed pasteurized, sterilized, U.H.T.
1 large tin evaporated milk
1 large tin sweetened condensed milk
1 '3½ pint' tin of instant dried skim milk (e.g. Marvel)
full cream milk powder
skimmed dried milk powder
8 small tomatoes (450g)
60 g flour
60 g margarine
2 pints pasteurized milk
500 cm³ (15 oz can) tomato juice
salt
pepper

Method
1 Comparison of different milks
For these experiments use a selection of the following milks; pasteurized, homogenized, skimmed, sterilized, U.H.T.,

evaporated, sweetened condensed, instant dried. The last three should be reconstituted as directed before they are used.

a *Effect of milk on the quality of tea.* Make a large pot of tea and pour the tea into 8 cups or beakers containing the same amount of the different cold milks. Sugar may be added if liked, but the same amount must be added to each sample. Observe any differences in colour, smell and taste.

b *Effect of milk on the quality of coffee.* Prepare small cups of coffee using the same amount of boiled milk and coffee powder for each type of milk (approx. 100 cm^3 milk and 1 level teaspoon of coffee). Add sugar to taste, but again add the same amount to each sample. Observe any differences in colour, smell and taste.

c *Effect of milk on the quality of cocoa.* Repeat **b** using cocoa or drinking chocolate.

d *Effect of milk on the quality of custard.* Prepare small samples of custard using the same amounts of the different milks, sugar and custard powder for each sample (approx. 100 cm^3 milk and 5g custard powder). Observe any differences in colour, smell, taste and texture.

e *Effect of milk on the quality of junket.* Warm about 100 cm^3 of each milk to 40°C and add a few drops of essence of rennet to each. Stir well and allow to cool. Observe any differences in texture between the samples and taste them. Try to account for the different textures.

From your results in this experiment, what are the advantages and disadvantages of the different milks used?

2 **Methods of using dried milks**
For these experiments compare a selection of dried milks; instantised dried milk in granules, full cream milk powder, skimmed milk powder, dried baby milks.

a *Reconstitution of dried milk.* For each sample of milk put 1 heaped desertspoonful of the dried milk product into a 150 cm^3 beaker and add water as follows;
 (i) add 100 cm^3 cold water and stir well
 (ii) add 100 cm^3 boiling water and stir well
 (iii) add 100 cm^3 warm water (60°C) and stir well
 (v) mix to a paste with 20 cm^3 cold water, stir well and add 80 cm^3 boiling water. Stir again. Compare the ease of mixing of the four methods and the appearance of the final products.

From your results what do you consider to be the best method of making up dried milk for use in the kitchen?

3 **Preparation of tomato products**
Measure the pH of tomato juice with indicator paper.

a *Tomato soup.* Combine 100 cm^3 milk with 100 cm^3 tomato juice in the following ways;
 (i) add cold juice to cold milk, stir and heat gently
 (ii) add cold juice to hot milk, stir and heat gently
(iii) add hot juice to cold milk, stir and heat gently
(iv) add hot juice to hot milk and stir well.
 Observe carefully which of the samples curdle.

What are the 2 factors responsible for curdling in making tomato soup?

b *Tomato Sauce.* For each sample use approx. 150 cm^3 milk, 15g margarine, 15g flour, 2 small tomatoes (100g), 50 cm^3 tomato juice, salt and pepper (same for each).
Skin tomatoes, chop finely and combine with the tomato juice.
Preparation of roux sauce: melt margarine, stir in the flour, cook for 1 minute, gradually stir in the liquid and continue cooking until a creamy texture is obtained.
 (i) prepare a hot milk roux sauce, mix with cold tomato and reheat.
 (ii) prepare a hot milk roux sauce, mix with hot tomato and reheat.
(iii) prepare a hot tomato roux sauce, mix with cold milk and reheat.
(iv) prepare a hot tomato roux sauce, mix with hot milk and reheat.
 Observe the colour, texture, taste and any curdling of the samples; which do you prefer?

Compare your results from **3 a** and **3 b** can you account for the differences?
What precautions would you suggest to prevent curdling in tomato soup and tomato sauce?

Questions

What is meant by the statement that all milk sold in Great Britain is TT?
Stewed rhubarb is very acid (pH3). What is likely to happen when you add hot custard or milk?
When requiring canned tomato soup (to which milk is added) for a picnic, would it be better to take it hot in a vacuum flask or cold and heat it just before serving? Give your reason.
Peas (pH6) are less acid than tomatoes. In what way does this make it easier to prepare pea soup than tomato soup?

Follow-up
Select three varieties of fresh milk and three types of preserved milk and compare them from the following points of view; (a) cost (b) nutritional value (c) method of storage (d) shelf life (time for which they can be stored in good condition) and (e) convenience value.

5 Dairy products I–cream, butter and curds

Aims
1 To compare the properties of various creams available to the consumer.
2 To extract butter from milk and cream.
3 To investigate the composition of curds and whey.

Introduction
Cream contains more fat than milk but relatively less protein and carbohydrate. The fat content of cream varies from 12% for half-cream to 18% for single cream and as high as 55% for clotted cream. The table below gives some typical figures.

	Composition		
	% fat	% protein	% carbohydrate
Milk, fresh	4	3	5
Cream, single	21	2	3
Cream, double	48	1	2

The properties of cream vary with the fat content. For example, the ease with which it flows decreases as the fat content rises. The ease with which cream can be whipped also varies with fat content. Cream, like milk, is an emulsion but on whipping, air is incorporated giving the cream a light foamy texture. Whipped cream is an air-in-water foam consisting of air cells enclosed by a watery film containing fat and protein. During whipping the protein is partly denatured and the fat is partly solidified, thus giving stability to the foam structure. If cream is whipped too much the fat globules clump together and separate out as butter.

Commercial butter is made from cream by churning i.e. stirring. The churning process converts the cream from an oil-in-water emulsion into a water-in-oil emulsion and causes butter fat to separate out. Butter is required by law to contain at least 80% milk fat and not more than 16% water. It is customary to add salt to butter to improve flavour and to act as a preservative; colour may also be added.

Churning and the consequent separation of butter fat is one way of converting cream into a solid product. Cream (and milk) can also be converted into a solid form by coagulating milk proteins using rennet; the product is known as curd and the liquid remaining is called whey. The production of curd is the first step in making cheese (see unit 6). When milk is converted into curd some of the nutrients of milk, such as water-soluble vitamins and minerals, are lost and remain in the whey. In the last part of this unit simple tests are used to find out which nutrients remain in the curd and which pass into the whey. As this is not a chemistry book the details of these tests are not given; you can regard them as colour indicators that show the presence or absence of a particular nutrient.

Required
Equipment:
basins or small bowls
rotary or hand whisks
can opener
stoppered 250 cm^3 conical flasks
muslin cloths for filtering
glass stirring rods
small flat dishes or tiles
large beakers (400 cm^3)
evaporating dishes
test tubes and bunsen burners
thermometer (0-110°C)
Materials:
1 small carton or can of different creams, e.g. single, double, whipping and coffee – all pasteurized
canned sterilized cream and half cream
evaporated milk
UHT cream and half cream
1 pint pasteurized milk
1 pint Channel Island pasteurized milk
rennet
Millon's reagent (mercury in nitric acid)
Fehlings solutions I and II (I is copper sulphate, II is alkaline tartrate)

Method
1 Properties of creams

a *Colour, taste and texture.* Take a small sample of the different creams and note any variation in colour. Stir each cream with a clean glass rod and note any variation in the texture and viscosity of the cream by comparing how easily each cream sticks to the glass rod and how quickly any surplus cream drops off the rod when it is removed from the cream. Taste each cream and compare the textures or feel of the different creams on the tongue and also the flavour.
From your results conclude;
 (i) how viscosity is related to the fat content of the cream (the less the cream flows, the higher is its viscosity);
 (ii) how the type of heat treatment given to the cream affects its flavour (see the introduction to unit 4 for description of treatments given).

b *Whipping quality.* Transfer the remainder of the cream to separate small bowls and whip until they are as thick as possible.
Note. If whipping cream is not available prepare a sample yourself by diluting a certain volume of double cream with 1/3 the volume of pasteurized milk.
From your results record which samples produce the best and worst whipped cream.

What is the danger of over-whipping double cream?
Why do you think whipping cream is so called?

Follow up
If whipped cream is warmed the foam structure callapses as the fat melts. What conditions of temperature do you think would be best (a) to whip cream and (b) to store it?

Can you suggest a simple practical procedure to check if your conclusions are correct? If time permits carry out this experiment and note your results.

2 Extraction of butter fat

Transfer the cream layer from ordinary pasteurized milk and Channel Island pasteurized milk (which has a higher fat content than ordinary milk) to separate 250 cm^3 conical flasks and stopper tightly. Shake the flasks well and observe any changes that occur while the butter fat is being extracted. When the lumps of yellow fat appear on the surface continue shaking for a few more minutes and then strain through a muslin cloth. Retain the liquid which drains through; this is buttermilk.

Compare the colour, flavour and texture of the butter-milk with the milk remaining in the bottle. Can you explain any differences?

Transfer the two butter fat samples to small dishes or tiles and taste them. Add a pinch of salt to each, stir well and mould into a small pat. Taste the samples and note which is the larger. Account for the differences in colour, taste and size between the two samples.

If possible repeat this experiment using samples of single, double and canned sterilized cream, and compare the resulting butters with those obtained from milk.

Can you think of any reason which makes it difficult to extract the butter fat from certain types of milk or cream?

Why is salt added to butter?

3 Separation of curds and whey

a *Making curds and whey.* The production of curds and whey is a preliminary stage in the manufacture of cheese and this experiment shows what happens to the nutrients of milk when milk is converted into cheese.

Pour about 200 cm^3 of the milk remaining from part **2** into a large beaker and warm gently to about 40°C. Stir it well and add 5 cm^3 essence of rennet before leaving to stand for 15 minutes. When the contents have set, break up the junket by stirring, noticing how this alters the texture. Warm the contents to 40°C again, stir well and strain through a muslin cloth retaining both the solid part (curds) and the liquid (whey).

Test the curd by rubbing a small piece between the fingers. Note what it feels and looks like. Is it greasy? Test the whey by tasting it; also note its colour. How does it differ from ordinary milk?

b *Testing for nutrients in curds and whey.*

(i) Milk contains the sugar lactose which can be detected by the simple Fehlings test. Therefore by testing both the curds and the whey using this test we can find out what has happened to the lactose.

In order to find out what a positive result in the Fehlings test looks like, try out the test on a lactose solution by taking 5 cm^3 in a test tube and adding 2 cm^3 of Fehlings solutions I and II. Shake and warm gently until a red coloured precipitate appears.

Test a small portion of curds by breaking it up and adding 2 cm^3 of Fehlings solutions I and II, shaking well and warming gently. Observe any colour changes. Repeat the test with a small portion of whey. Where has most of the lactose gone and how does this affect the carbohydrate content of cheese?

(ii) The main protein in milk — see unit 3 — is caseinogen and its presence can be tested using Millon's reagent with which it gives a pink-red coloured precipitate on warming.

Break up a small piece of curd, place it in a test tube and add 2 cm^3 of Millon's reagent. Warm gently and observe any colour change. Repeat the test with a small portion of whey. Has the caseinogen originally present in the milk passed into the curds or the whey? How does this affect the protein content of cheese?

(iii) The other main proteins in milk are coagulated by heat — see unit 3, experiment 2 a. Pour some of the remaining whey into an evaporating dish and warm gently. Does a skin form? What do your results tell you about the proteins in whey? Continue heating the whey until it almost boils dry observing any changes in colour and smell. Leave the evaporating dish to cool and taste the crystals that appear. How is this connected with experiment (i) above?

What causes liquid milk to turn into a solid cheese? When curd (or cheese) is made from milk what nutrients are lost?

Follow up

Obtain samples of cottage cheese and Cheddar cheese and compare the appearance, taste and texture of these with your sample of curds. Check the food value of the two cheeses from McCance and Widdowson's *Composition of foods* (HMSO) or *Manual of Nutrition* (HMSO). Would you expect the food value of curds to be more like that of cottage cheese or Cheddar cheese? Give your reasons.

6 Dairy products II–cheese

Aims

1 To compare the behaviour of different cheeses when cooked.
2 To investigate some properties of processed cheeses.

Introduction

Cheese is made from pasteurized ripened (sour) milk by coagulating the milk proteins with rennet. The solid curd formed is treated in various ways to allow the whey to escape and to develop texture and flavour. A typical hard cheese such as Cheddar contains about 35% water compared to 87% water in the milk from which it is made. This indicates that cheese is a concentrated food and Cheddar cheese is about 1/3 fat and 1/4 protein and is also rich in calcium, phosphorus and vitamin A.

As cheese is rich in fat and protein, the aims in cooking cheese are to prevent the fat from separating out and the protein from becoming over-coagulated and so stringy and tough. This means that it is best to use low temperatures and short cooking times in cheese cookery. The same principle applies in making cheese sauces which should have a creamy smooth texture. Over-cooking of such sauces may cause the proteins to over-coagulate producing curdling and a stringy texture.

The properties of cheese may be modified by the addition of salts which act as emulsifying agents. This is done during the preparation of processed cheese, and it results in the cheese having a smooth soft texture; it also prevents fat from separating out. The processing of cheese improves cooking quality by creating a stable emulsion from which fat does not separate easily and the salts added also raise pH and this has the effect of making casein more soluble and less likely to form a tough texture on cooking.

Required

Equipment:
pans and wooden spoons
small cups or beakers
sharp knives
cheese graters
test tubes
bunsen burners
gas rings
grill

Materials:
small samples (about 150g) of a wide variety of cheeses e.g. Cheshire, Lancashire, Leicester, Edam, Danish Blue
300g Cheddar cheese
150g processed cheese
packet of cheese spread portions
sliced bread
4 pints pasteurized milk
150g plain flour
150g margarine or butter
salt
pepper
sodium citrate
disodium phosphate
cream of tartar

Method

1 The behaviour of cheese on cooking

a *Effect of heat on cheese.* Grate a small sample of Cheddar cheese and processed cheese into the bottom of separate test tubes. Warm gently over a bunsen burner observing carefully what happens as the cheese becomes liquid. Allow the cheese to bubble for 2-3 minutes and then leave the test tube to cool. Note the appearance and texture of the cheese when cool.

How has heating affected the texture of the cheese?
Is there any difference in the behaviour of the 2 cheeses?

b *Grilled cheese.* Toast several slices of bread lightly on both sides. Cut each slice in half and divide about 30g of grated cheese equally between the two halves. Use a variety of cheeses including; Cheddar, Lancashire, a blue cheese, processed cheese and cheese spread. Grill both halves under a hot grill until the cheese just turns liquid, remove one half but continue heating the other half for 3-5 minutes until over-grilled.
Compare the appearance, texture and flavour of the half-slices of each cheese. Which has the best appearance, texture and flavour?

Cheese is a concentrated food — it takes a pint of milk to produce 60g cheese.

A selection of cheeses.

Which types of cheese are suitable for making cheese on toast and what would you suggest as a suitable grilling time?

c *Cheeses suitable for sauce making.* Prepare approximately 1 pint of a basic white sauce using 1 pint of milk, 30g plain flour, 30g margarine, seasoned with salt and pepper. Divide between 4 or 5 small cups or beakers and while still hot stir in 30g finely grated cheese. Use different cheeses e.g. Cheddar, Leicester, Edam and a blue cheese and compare the different textures, colours and flavours.

Which cheese makes the best cheese sauce?

d *Methods of making cheese sauce.* For each method make approximately 1/4 pint sauce using 1/4 pint milk, 7g flour, 7g margarine or butter, seasoning, 7g cheese.
 (i) Combine the fat, flour and milk by the roux method (see Unit 4) and add the cheese, finely grated, after removing the completed sauce from the heat.
 (ii) Combine the fat, flour and milk as in (i) but add the grated cheese at the beginning with the fat and flour.
 (iii) Boil the milk, add the fat and then thicken with flour made into a paste with a little milk. Add the grated cheese after removing the completed sauce from the heat.
 (iv) Boil the milk with grated cheese added at the beginning, then add the fat and thicken with a flour paste as above.

Compare the flavour, appearance and texture of the four cheese sauces and decide which is the best method for making cheese sauce. Give your reasons.

2 Processed cheeses
Prepare approximately 1 pint basic white sauce as in **1 c** above dividing it equally between 6 small cups or beakers. While still hot stir in 30g grated cheese as indicated below;
 (i) Cheddar cheese
 (ii) Cheddar cheese plus about 1g disodium phosphate
 (iii) Cheddar cheese plus about 1 g sodium citrate
 (iv) Cheddar cheese plus about 1g cream of tartar
 (v) Processed cheese
 (vi) Cheese spread
Stir well and compare the textures and flavours of each.

How do the 3 salts used modify the nature of Cheddar cheese?
What advantages has processed cheese in cooking?

Follow up
Find a store with a good selection of cheeses and make a selection including a hard cheese, a cream cheese, a blue cheese, a processed cheese and a cheese spread. Note the cost and weight of each, check their food value from tables such as McCance and Widdowson's *Composition of foods* (HMSO), and compare their cost per unit weight with their nutrient content.
   Which of the cheeses would you use (a) to make cheese sandwiches (b) in a cheese salad (c) to make a cheese sauce and (d) for grilling on toast? Give your reasons.

7 Eggs I–structure and composition

Aims

1 To investigate the structure of an egg and analyse some of the nutrients present.
2 To show the effect of heat on both the white and yolk of an egg.
3 To note the changes that take place in an egg as it gets older.

Introduction

A hen's egg has 3 distinct parts; shell, yolk and white (see diagram). The function of the shell is to protect the contents and it is therefore made of a hard material — calcium carbonate — that does not dissolve in water. It is affected by acids however, which dissolve it and produce carbon dioxide gas that turns lime water milky. The shell is porous because it contains tiny holes which allow gases to pass through. A fresh egg contains only a small air pocket but as it gets older air passes into it and the pocket becomes bigger. As bacteria as well as air can pass through the shell, eggs deteriorate on storage. The freshness of an egg can be gauged from the size of the air pocket, because as the air pocket increases the buoyancy of the egg increases; thus the older an egg is the nearer the surface it will float if put into a solution of salt.

Just inside the shell are two thin membranes that separate the shell from the white and enclose the air space. The white of egg is a viscous colourless liquid being mainly water (88%) together with some protein (11%) and small amounts of mineral salts and riboflavine. The physical nature of the egg white varies with the freshness of the egg. In a fresh egg there are clearly defined areas of thin white and thick white, whereas in an old egg the white is thinner. The quality of egg white can be found by breaking the egg into a clean plate (see diagram).

The yolk of an egg is suspended in the white and is held in position by the fibrous-like chalazae. The yolk is a more concentrated source of nutrients than the white and contains 48% water, 32% fat and 17% protein together with mineral elements and fat soluble vitamins. The fat of egg yolk is emulsified and so is easy to digest.

When eggs are heated they set, as protein in the white and yolk coagulate. This aspect is dealt with more fully in unit 9.

The internal structure of an egg

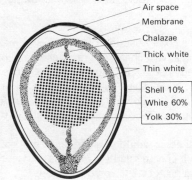

Air space
Membrane
Chalazae
Thick white
Thin white

Shell 10%
White 60%
Yolk 30%

Required

Equipment:
2 large beakers 400 cm^3
2 small beakers 100 cm^3
test tubes
electrical balance for accurate weighing
0-110°C thermometers
glass stirring rods
1 large container — e.g. mixing-bowl or large pan
2 large flat plates
3 small pans
3 small basins or bowls
hand or rotary whisk
large serving spoons
sharp knife
bunsen burners or gas rings
pH paper (Universal, pH 1-14)

Materials:
eggs — 9 Class A standard
2 Class A large
2 Class A medium
4 class B standard — at least 1 month old
4 Extra standard — very fresh new laid
1 pint milk
Millons reagent
Fehlings I and II
iodine in potassium iodide solution
dilute hydrochloric acid
sodium bicarbonate
lime water
salt
sugar
vinegar

Method

1 Structure and composition

a *Comparison of the weights of different sized eggs.* Weigh 2 large eggs on an accurate balance — if possible to the second place of decimals. Record the weight in grams. Carefully crack open the eggs and separate as accurately as possible the shell, white and yolk into 6 pre-weighed small beakers. Re-weigh the beakers and from these results work out the percentage shell, yolk and white in a large egg.
Repeat using standard and medium eggs.
(If desired this experiment could be done with more than 2 eggs of each size to obtain a better average value, or extended to include other sizes of egg).

Using the current price of these different sized eggs, work out which size gives the best value for money.

b *Composition of egg shell and nature of the internal structure.* Look at the shell from **a** to find the position of the membranes and air space. Put these shells in a glass beaker, cover with dilute hydrochloric acid and observe what happens. Can you explain this reaction? What has happened to the egg shell membranes? If desired some of the gas given off could be collected and tested with lime water in order to further identify the components of the shell.

Repeat this experiment with a raw egg still inside its shell, until all the shell has been removed and the egg is just enclosed in the membranes. Carefully rinse the egg in cold water and notice the presence of the air space and the yolk. Why has some of the white changed from being clear to opaque? Choose the clearest part of the egg and rotate it carefully looking for the germ or embryo and the chalazae.

c *Testing for the presence of nutrients in egg white and egg yolk.* Test small portions of the white and yolk remaining from a above
 (i) *for protein* using Millon's reagent looking for a red colour on warming for a positive result;
 (ii) *for sugar* using Fehling's solution I & II looking for a brick red colour on warming for a positive result;
 (iii) *for starch* using iodine in potassium iodide solution looking for a blue/black colour for a positive result.

What does this tell you about the presence of protein, sugar and carbohydrate in the white and yolk of egg?

2 Effect of heat on an egg

a *Coagulation temperature of egg white, egg yolk and whole egg.* Fill 3 test tubes to a depth of 3 cm with raw egg white, raw yolk, and raw whole egg. Put the test tubes in a large beaker of water and slowly heat stirring the egg all the time. Record the temperature at which each coagulates. Which coagulates first, the yolk or the white? Why?

b *Effect of added substances on the coagulation temperature.* Repeat a with the addition of a small amount of milk to each of the 3 test tubes and note the new coagulation temperature.
Repeat again using vinegar, sugar and sodium bicarbonate. Can you explain these differences in coagulation temperatures?

Can you suggest why vinegar is sometimes added to the water in which eggs are poached, and why sodium bicarbonate never is?

3 Effect of ageing on an egg
For all these experiments use eggs which are very fresh and repeat with eggs that are fairly fresh, at least a month old and even older if possible.

a Fill a large container with 10% salt solution and add the eggs to it. Note whether the eggs touch the bottom, float near the bottom, half way up the container, near the surface or actually break the surface of the solution. How can you account for these differences?

b Carefully break the eggs out onto a clean flat plate and compare the shape and height of the yolks, the proportion

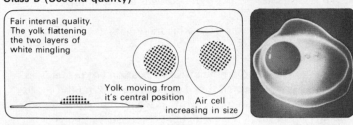

Class A (First quality)

Excellent internal quality and has three distinct parts: the yolk, a clear translucent white of a gelatinous consistency and an outer layer of thin white

Yolk central

A small air cell

Class B (Second quality)

Fair internal quality. The yolk flattening the two layers of white mingling

Yolk moving from it's central position

Air cell increasing in size

Class C (Third quality)

Suitable for the manufacture of foodstuffs for human consumption, but which are not on sale in shops

Egg quality as defined by EEC regulations

of thick and thin white, and the area taken up by the egg as a whole.
What causes these changes?

c Look into the empty shells and compare sizes of air cells.

d Measure the pH of the whites and yolks of the different eggs using pH paper. What must have happened to cause this change?

e Boil the eggs for about 10 mins., cool and shell carefully, Slice in half lengthways and notice the position of the yolk, whether it has broken through the white, any colour change and also the size of the air space.

f Poach the eggs in simmering water in individual pans of water for approx. 4 mins. Remove the eggs and compare their texture, shape and taste.

g Whip up raw egg whites and compare the ease of whipping, the foam stiffness and stability.

What are the disadvantages of eggs which have been stored at room temperature for a long time?
If possible compare a month old egg which has been stored in a refrigerator with one left at room temperature — and then deduce which is the better way of storing eggs.

Follow up
1 Find out as much as you can about the way in which the quality of eggs is tested commercially.
What does the term candling mean?
2 Visit several stores and find out as much as you can about the quality of the eggs being sold from the information on the outside of the package. Now that the U.K. is in the European Economic Community (EEC) eggs sold in the U.K. should comply with EEC regulations.

8 Eggs II–simple egg cookery

Aims
1 To apply the principle of heat coagulation of proteins to boiled eggs.
2 To investigate the effect of additives on the nature of poached eggs.
3 To find the best way of making meringues.

Introduction
Egg cookery is based on the effect of heat on egg proteins; as these proteins are heated they coagulate so causing the egg to set. The main protein of egg white is *albumin* and it is found that egg white starts to coagulate at about 60°C. Egg yolk does not coagulate as easily as the white, and coagulation is not appreciable until about 70°C. The rate of coagulation increases as the temperature is raised. Apart from temperature, coagulation is also affected by pH and added salts. The addition of acid, with consequent lowering of pH, and the addition of salts promotes the coagulation of protein.

When eggs are hard boiled a greenish ring may be formed around the yolk; this is caused by the action of iron (from the yolk) and sulphur combining to form iron sulphide.

On beating, egg white becomes stiff due to partial coagulation of the albumin. If this beaten egg white is heated, more coagulation occurs and the egg white becomes rigid. During beating the protein becomes stretched out in the form of a thin film that encloses air in the form of tiny bubbles. The light foam structure thus formed becomes solid on heating as albumin coagulates further. The stability of the foam is affected not only by temperature but also by the addition of other substances. For instance, the presence of acid or sugar increases stability whereas the presence of water or fat decreases stability. Even a trace of fat mixed with egg white is sufficient to cause the foam to collapse.

Required

Equipment:
5 saucepans
6 small frying pans or omelette pans for poaching
serving spoons, sharp knives, teaspoons
8 small bowls or basins
hand or rotary whisks
baking trays or sheets
gas burners
gas or electric oven
5 thermometers 0-110°C

Materials:
2 dozen standard eggs (or 16 eggs + 8 whites of egg)
sugar
vinegar
salt
sodium bicarbonate
lemon juice
cream of tartar
cooking oil

Beaten egg white has a light, foamy structure.

Method
1 Boiled eggs
Cook 2 eggs by each of the methods below, plunging one egg into cold running water immediately after removing from the cooking water and leaving the other egg to cool naturally at room temperature:

a vigorously boiling water (100°C) for 10 minutes

b vigorously boiling water (100°C) for 30 minutes

c simmer at 90°C for 20 minutes

d water held at 80°C for 40 minutes

e water held at 70°C for 60 minutes

When all the eggs are cold, shell carefully and slice in half lengthways. Compare the texture of the whites and yolks and also the colour of the yolks for the different eggs. Can you account for these differences?

For the eggs cooked by methods (a) and (b) carefully remove the yolks from the whites and notice whether or not there is a greenish grey surface line round the yolks. From the above results, what recommendations should be made as to the best method of hard boiling eggs without producing discolouration around the yolk?

2 Poached eggs

Using the shallow frying/omelette pans, bring some water up to simmering point and then poach 1 egg in each for approximately 5 minutes until done — adding the following substances to the water before cracking each egg:

a no addition (control)

b 3 drops vinegar

c 1 teaspoon vinegar

d pinch salt

e pinch of sodium bicarbonate

f ½ teaspoon lemon juice

Remove all eggs from the water when done and compare the shape, texture, appearance, colour and taste of the different eggs. Why do these differences occur? What recommendations should be made about the poaching of eggs?

From these two experiments discuss the reasons for adding salt to the water when *boiling* eggs.

3 Meringues — and foam stability

For the following series of experiments take 1 egg white and beat it up to a stiff foam after adding the substance indicated:

a no addition (control)

b 10 cm^3 cold water

c 1g cream of tartar

d 1g salt

e 10g sugar (1 level tbs)

f 2 cm^3 vinegar (½ tsp)

g 2 cm^3 egg yolk (½ tsp)

After whisking, a meringue mixture should be a stiff but smooth foam with a glossy appearance.

Compare the ease of beating and the stiffness of the final foam. Leave for 15 minutes and then compare the foam stiffness again. Which is the more stable foam? Which additives increase / decrease foam stability? Re-whip the egg whites to a stiff foam where possible and fold in approximately 30g of sugar. Spoon onto a baking sheet and cook in a cool oven until dried out. Remove from oven and compare texture, shape and taste of the meringue. What recommendations would you make about making meringues?

In making meringues it is important that not even a trace of yolk gets into the egg white. Why is this? It is said that the addition of cream of tartar to a meringue mixture improves the whiteness of the meringue. From the results of your experiment would you say that this is true?

Follow up

In developing countries there is a shortage of animal protein, and an increasing consumption of eggs is desirable as a way of improving the quality and quantity of protein in the diet. Yet in a developing country such as India consumption of eggs per person is only 5 or 6 per year compared with 4 or 5 per week in Britain. Find out as much as you can about the nature of the diet in India and try and account for the low consumption of eggs. Can you suggest any methods of encouraging a higher consumption of eggs?

9 Eggs III–basic egg custards

Aims

1 To illustrate the use of an egg as a thickening agent when making custard.
2 To investigate the effect of recipe variation on the coagulation of egg custard.
3 To investigate the effect of temperature and conditions on the coagulation of egg custard.

Introduction

Egg cookery is based on the effect of heat on egg proteins as pointed out in unit 8. In making a baked custard the object is to control coagulation of egg proteins to produce a firm but smooth gel structure. Whole eggs start to coagulate at about 70°C but when other ingredients, such as milk and sugar are added as in making a baked custard, coagulation starts at a higher temperature (about 80°C). To achieve satisfactory results in making a baked custard temperature and cooking time should be just sufficient to coagulate the protein. If the temperature is too high or the cooking time too long protein is over coagulated resulting in a custard with a poor texture i.e. one that is porous containing large air bubbles and which separates easily, especially when cut. Over-heating may also cause curdling of milk proteins (see unit 3).

The proportions of the ingredients in a baked custard are important, and if the basic recipe is altered the cooking procedure may also need modifying while the character of the final product may be changed. For example, if an increased proportion of sugar is used the temperature at which coagulation occurs is raised and the flavour of the custard altered. On the other hand, if the proportion of egg is increased the coagulation temperature is lowered and the increased amount of egg protein present produces a firmer texture. If egg whites are used in place of whole egg, the coagulation temperature is lowered (see unit 8) and the colour of the custard changed. If the pH of the liquid custard mix is lowered by the addition of an acid substance, there will be an increased tendency for the milk to curdle. The changes produced by varying the proportions of ingredients in a baked custard recipe illustrate the need to understand the *functions* of each ingredient in a recipe.

A baked custard needs careful cooking to achieve the desired flavour and texture. Does it make any difference to the final product whether the containers stand in a water bath during cooking or not?

Required

Equipment:
2 ovens — one set at 175°C
one set at 250°C
gas or electric rings (or bunsen burners)
small pans or 500 cm³ beakers
shallow metal trays to fit in oven
small custard cups or foil pie cases
mixing bowls
egg whisks/beaters
thermometer 0-110°C

Materials:
7 pints pasteurized milk
15 eggs
450 g sugar
salt
1 lemon
10 g raisins
yellow food colouring

Method

1 **Basic egg custard recipe**
200 cm³ pasteurized milk (approx. 1/3 pint)
1 egg
25 g sugar
pinch salt
Warm the milk to about 60°C but do not allow it to boil. Beat the egg with the sugar and salt and stir in the warm milk. Divide the mixture into small custard cups and stand these in a shallow metal tray containing hot water. Bake in a cool oven (175°C) for about 40 mins. until the custards have set into a firm smooth gel. Remove from the oven and cool slightly before inspection.

Remove the custards from their containers and observe their shape, texture, appearance and taste.

How can you account for the change in texture that occurred during cooking and what role have the milk proteins played in this change?

2 Variations in ingredient proportions

Make 8 custards exactly as in **1** but with the following modifications:

a Omit the sugar from the basic recipe

b Use twice as much sugar, i.e. 50 g

c Use 2 egg whites instead of 1 whole egg

d Use 2 egg yolks instead of 1 whole egg

e Use 2 whole eggs instead of 1

f Use twice as much milk, i.e. 400 cm^3

g Add the juice of a lemon or a few slices of lemon

h Add a few raisins, approx. 10 g

Cook all the custards in the oven for exactly the same length of time (about 40 mins.) as for the basic recipe. Cool the custards and observe any differences in their shape, texture, colour, appearance, and taste. In particular notice which custards have begun to curdle and in which custards air bubbles spoil the texture.

What is the effect of sugar on the texture of the custard? Could a variation in the baking *time* overcome these changes — and if so how?
How do you account for the difference in texture and taste for the custards made with either 2 whites or 2 yolks?
Do you think the "whites only" modification makes an acceptable custard?
If there is time repeat this modification using a few drops of yellow food colouring.
What sort of fruit could be incorporated into an egg custard mix? Give reasons for your answer.

3 Effects of temperature

Make up a further 5 custards as in **1** but use different temperatures as follows:

a Use cold milk instead of pre-warmed milk

b *Boil* the milk first and then pour onto egg/sugar mix

c Bake the custard in a cool oven at 175°C without the water bath.

d Bake the custard in a hot oven at 250°C with a water bath.

e Bake the custard in a hot oven at 250°C without a water bath.

Cool the custards and again compare their appearance, texture and taste with custard made using the basic recipe method.
(If necessary modifications **c, d** and **e** could be incorporated into either Experiment **1** or **2** by using small custard cups and baking them under four different oven conditions).

What is the effect of baking the custards at a higher temperature?
Why is it best to bake the custard while it stands in a tray of hot water (or a bain marie)? How does this procedure affect the coagulation rate of the custard?

Follow up

Soufflés (see photograph) are similar in some ways to baked custards, but they differ in texture — the soufflé being light and fluffy and the baked custard being smooth and jelly-like. Find out how the method of making soufflés differs from that of making baked custards and account for the difference in texture.

A souffle, showing how it rises during baking to give it a light, fluffy texture.

10 Meat and fish cookery

Aims
1 To compare the loss in weight of fish and different meats when cooked using dry heat.
2 To compare how fish and meat behave on boiling.
3 To investigate the nature of the changes occurring in fish and meat when they are cooked.

Introduction
Lean meat is the muscle tissue of animals and it consists of long, thread-like fibres held together by connective tissue to form bundles. Muscle tissue is about ¾ water, ¼ protein together with small amounts of 'invisible' fat, mineral elements and vitamins, notably of the B group. Meat as bought also contains variable amounts of visible fat.

The behaviour of the proteins in meat is of prime importance in meat cookery. Muscle fibres contain the proteins *myosin* and *actin*, while connective tissue contains the proteins *collagen* and *elastin*. On heating, the proteins are denatured to an extent, that depends on the cooking temperature and this causes the meat to shrink and liquid to be squeezed out. In moist heat cooking methods, this 'juice' — which contains soluble proteins, mineral salts, vitamins and flavouring substances, — passes into the cooking liquid. This is not important, however, when the cooking liquid is incorporated in the final dish, as in stews and casseroles, or used for making a sauce or gravy. The amount of 'juice' lost from meat increases as the cooking time increases.

In dry heat cooking, water reaching the surface as a result of protein shrinkage evaporates, leaving behind the non-volatile flavouring substances. This process leaves the meat surface dry but with a good flavour. Dry heat cooking also leads to loss of drippings, mainly of melted fat.

A microwave oven in which meat could be cooked.

When meat is cooked collagen is converted into soft, soluble gelatin and this is an important factor in increasing tenderness; elastin also softens on cooking but not to the same extent as collagen. Tough meat is best cooked slowly at low temperatures and for this reason it is often stewed.

The colour of meat changes on cooking and this is largely due to changes in the main pigment in meat called *myoglobin*. When meat is cut the freshly cut surface is purplish-red but in air the myoglobin is converted to an oxidised form, which is bright red. On cooking, changes in the myoglobin cause the colour to change to brown.

Fish undergoes similar changes to meat when it is cooked. It contains less connective tissue than meat and no elastin and so cooking is intended to make it palatable rather than to improve tenderness. In dry heat cooking soluble proteins are coagulated and some shrinkage and loss of liquid by evaporation occurs. In moist heat cooking soluble nutrients and flavouring materials are lost to the cooking liquor making the fish rather tasteless. Cooking of fish is complete when it readily forms flakes.

Required

Equipment:
oven
small trays or foil dishes to fit in oven
250 cm^3 beakers
0-110°C thermometers
bunsen burners
tripods
gauzes
balance

Materials:
Approximately 200 g each of the following:
beef steak
minced beef
pork
lamb chop
fish (e.g. cod)

Method
1 **To investigate the weight loss in different meats and fish when cooked in an oven**
Preheat the oven to 175°C (or 350°F or gas mark 4). Weight out about 100 g of the different meats and the fish as accurately as you can, noting the weight of each. If possible include a piece of meat containing a bone to see whether this affects the cooking loss. Transfer the weighed samples to separate trays and cook in the oven for 30 minutes. Remove from the oven and when completely cool, reweigh each sample in a clean container, discarding any of the meat juices extracted during cooking.
Note the appearance and texture of the fish sample after cooking.

Calculation. Work out the per cent loss in weight during cooking for each sample as follows:

$$\% \text{ loss in weight} = \frac{\text{loss in weight}}{\text{original weight}} \times 100$$

$$= \frac{\text{original weight - final weight}}{\text{original weight}} \times 100$$

Which sample shows the greatest % loss on cooking? Does the presence of bone in meat seem to make much difference to weight loss? How do you explain the relatively high weight loss occurring in all types of meat when cooked in an oven?

Lean fish such as haddock and cod contain much less fat than meat. Do you consider cooking in an oven to be a suitable method for such fish? Give your reasons. Why are lean fish often cooked by frying?

2 To investigate how different meats and fish behave on boiling

a *Effect of using water heated from cold.* Weigh about 50 g samples of fish and different meats as accurately as possible and transfer then to separate beakers containing 150 cm^3 of cold water. Gently warm each beaker with a bunsen burner recording the temperature of the water at regular intervals. Observe carefully any changes in the appearance of the sample or the cooking water including changes in colour, amount of extracted solids and any scum formation; also note the temperature at which these changes occur. Continue heating the sample until the water boils and then simmer for a further 5 minutes, again observing any changes. Finally remove the sample from the water, drain off surplus water and when completely cool reweigh in a clean container.

Calculate the % weight loss in each sample as in experiment **1**.

What difference do you think it would make if the cooked samples were weighed hot rather than cold? Give your reason.

Can you explain the changes that you observed during the cooking process and why there may be a danger of the water boiling over?

Compare the behaviour of the cooking water in this experiment with the changes observed when milk is heated to boiling in a pan.

b *Effect of cooking in boiling water.* Weigh about 50 g samples of fish and different meats as accurately as possible and transfer them to a separate beaker containing about 150 cm^3 of boiling water.

Addition of the samples takes the water off the boil; continue heating until the water boils again and then for a further 10 minutes. Note the changes in the appearance of the samples and in the cooking water as in **a**.

Remove the samples from the water, drain off surplus water and when cool reweigh in a clean container and calculate the weight loss of each sample as before.

Can you explain the changes that you observed? How do you account for the differences between meat cooked in water heated from cold and meat cooked in boiling water?

c *Comparison of cooked meats.* Take the samples of each meat cooked by the three different methods (i.e. oven, water from cold and boiling water), cut them in half (unless minced) and compare them for colour, flavour and texture.

From the above comparison which method of cooking do you consider to be most suitable for;
(i) a large joint of pork
(ii) a piece of boiled ham,
(iii) minced beef for a curry or stew?
Give your reasons.

Follow up

1 Find out as much as you can about the use of pressure cookers and microwave ovens for cooking meat. How would you expect steaks cooked by grilling to differ from steaks cooked in a microwave oven?

2 Meat is sometimes roasted after it has been wrapped in aluminium foil. Find out what effect this has on flavour and colour compared with ordinary roasting. What are advantages and disadvantages of this technique?

3 From the results of your experiment and from any additional information you can find, write down as many differences between meat cookery and fish cookery as you can.

11 Meat – methods of tenderisation

Aims

1 To investigate whether tough meat can be made more tender purely by mechanical treatment.

2 To investigate whether tough meat can be made more tender by altering the hydration of the meat proteins.

3 To compare the effectiveness of various proteolytic enzymes for tenderisation of meat.

4 To discover the most efficient way of using a commercial meat tenderising salt.

Introduction

Meat is cooked for a number of reasons, one of the most important of which is to make it tender. Tough meat is difficult to tenderise by cooking alone mainly because it contains a high proportion of connective tissue. In connective tissue there is an insoluble protein — elastin — which softens only a little on cooking (see unit 10). It is important therefore to find additional ways of improving the tenderness of tough meat apart from cooking.

Tough meat contains relatively large amounts of connective tissue and meat may be tenderised by breaking down this tissue mechanically. This may be done by pounding the meat with a spoon or meat hammer, by breaking up connective tissue by scoring the meat surface with a sharp knife or by chopping or mincing the meat into small pieces.

The tenderness of meat can be improved during cooking by the addition of salt or an acid substance to lower pH. Lowering of pH increases the rate at which insoluble collagen of connective tissue is converted into soluble gelatin. Addition of salt has a similar effect, though care must be taken as to how much is added, as an excess of salt denatures and toughens protein. Elastin is unaffected by the addition of a salt or acid.

Meat can be made more tender by the use of enzymes or commercial preparations containing enzymes known as *meat tenderisers.* Just as certain enzymes in the digestive tract assist in the breakdown of protein during digestion, so similar enzymes can be used to break down meat protein and improve tenderness. Proteolytic enzymes — that is enzymes which break down protein — act by splitting the peptide links that join the amino acids making up the protein chain. Tenderisers can be injected into an animal just before it is killed or they may be added to the surface of the meat or cooking liquor before cooking. Care must be taken not to use too much tenderiser for not only is the tough connective tissue broken down but also too much muscle tissue, so making the meat soft and mushy.

A number of enzymes are suitable for tenderising meat. For example, *bromelin* obtained from pineapples and *ficin* obtained from figs are both used, also the enzyme *trypsin.* Enzymes, being themselves proteins, are very sensitive to temperature. Plant enzymes work best at about $25^{\circ}C$ while animal enzymes work best at about $37^{\circ}C$. All enzyme activity is destroyed on boiling and even much lower temperatures may soon inactivate them. This means that cooking processes destroy the tenderising action of enzymes, and to be effective tenderisers must be given time to act before cooking commences.

Papain (pronounced pap-ay-in) obtained from the juice of papaya fruit is particularly useful as a tenderiser because it retains its enzyme activity at higher temperatures than other enzymes. It works best at $55-75^{\circ}C$.

Required

Equipment:
250 cm^3 beakers
bunsen burners
tripods and gauzes
sharp knife
wooden spoon or wooden meat tenderising hammer
10 and 100 cm^3 measuring cylinders
thermometer $0-110^{\circ}C$

Materials:
1000 g tough lean meat e.g. beef
500 g minced beef
vinegar
salt
cheap wine
lemon juice
trypsin — or other digestive proteolytic enzyme
papain
commercial meat tenderising salts (e.g. McCormicks)

Method

1 **Mechanical tenderisation of meat**

Take approx. 200 g of lean beef and cut it into 4 equally sized pieces. Treat as follows:

a Control sample. No treatment.

b Beat the meat well with the back of the wooden spoon or meat hammer.

c Score the surface of the meat with a sharp knife.

d Chop the meat into approx. 8 smaller pieces.

Also take 50 g of minced beef as a fifth sample.

Place each sample of meat in a 250 cm^3 beaker containing approx. 100 cm^3 of cold water and leave to soak for 5 mins. Gently warm all the beakers to $80^{\circ}C$ and simmer for 15 mins. taking care not to let the water boil over. Drain off the water and cool the meat samples. Examine each sample carefully and look for any changes in the fibrous structure of the meat as compared with the control. Try to assess any difference in texture first of all by feeling the pieces of meat or pulling the fibres apart and then taste the meat and compare the 'chewability' of the different samples.

This experiment may be repeated with similar samples of meat put into boiling water and then simmered for 15 mins.

to see whether the tenderisation effect is more or less pronounced at a higher temperature.

How can you explain the effect that these mechanical treatments have on the tenderness of the meats?

2 Hydration of meat protein

Note. *The water holding capacity of a piece of meat may be increased by the addition of a small amount of salt or by lowering the pH with the addition of an acid substance.* Take 6 equal sized 50 g samples of lean meat and place them in 250 cm^3 beakers containing approx. 100 cm^3 cold water. Make the following additions:

a control sample — no additions

b 5 cm^3 vinegar

c 5 cm^3 lemon juice

d 5 cm^3 wine

e 2 g salt

f 20 g salt

Prepare a parallel set of six beakers each containing approx. 50 g minced beef with the same additions as above. Leave each sample to soak for at least 5 mins. and then gently warm to 80°C and simmer for 15 mins. Drain off the water, cool and examine the samples of meat as in experiment **1** comparing all the samples with the control.

Again this experiment may be repeated using meat samples put into boiling water instead of cold water and then simmered for 15 minutes.

Does the addition of salt or acids have any effect on the tenderness of the meat? If so which do you consider to be the most effective?
Can you explain the reason for the differences between the tenderness of the samples cooked in 2 g salt and 20 g salt?
What is a marinade? Why is marinading a useful method for cooking tough meat?

3 Meat tenderising enzymes

Take 5 equally sized 50 g samples of lean meat and place them in 250 cm^3 beakers containing approx. 100 cm^3 cold water and the following additions:

a control sample — no additions

b 2 g trypsin

c 10 g trypsin

d 2 g papain

e 10 g papain

Alternatively try any other proteolytic enzymes as available. Leave each sample to soak for at least 5 mins. and then warm gently to 80°C and simmer for 15 mins. Drain off the water, cool and examine each sample as in experiment **1** comparing all samples with the control.

Have these enzymes had any effect on the tenderness of the meat? If so which was the most effective? What is the effect of using larger amounts of the enzyme?

Follow up

1 What is the optimum temperature of activity of the two enzymes trypsin and papain? Does this have any bearing on the results you have obtained?
2 From the results of experiments **2** and **3**, what would be the most suitable components of a commercial meat tenderising salt to be used by housewives?
3 Find as many different commerical meat tenderising salts as possible and examine the labels to see what the ingredients are. Identify which you think are the active ingredients and then comment on the reasons for including the other ingredients.

4 Use of commercial meat tenderising salts

Take 5 equally sized 50 g pieces of lean beef and place them in 250 cm^3 beakers. Treat the samples as follows:

a Rub 2 g tenderising salt into the meat surface and leave for 15 mins. Add 100 cm^3 cold water, heat to 80°C and simmer for 15 mins.

b Add 2 g tenderising salt and 100 cm^3 cold water to the meat. Leave to soak for 15 mins. and then heat to 80°C and simmer for 15 mins.

c Add 2 g tenderising salt and 100 cm^3 hot water (60°C) to the meat. Leave to soak for 15 mins., heat to 80°C and simmer for 15 mins.

d Rub 2 g tenderising salt into the meat surface, add 100 cm^3 boiling water and simmer for 15 mins.

Draw off the water, cool and examine the meat samples as before.

Which of these methods have been most successful for tenderising the meat? Can you explain why?

Further experiments could be done to look at the effect of increasing the amount of tenderising salt e.g. perform the above experiments using 10 g instead of 2 g, or using different times.

12 Flour–starch and protein components

Aims
1 To separate the starch and gluten components of different flours and to examine their properties.
2 To investigate the effect of various additives on the strength of gluten.
3 To investigate the effect of various additives on the gelatinisation of starch.

Introduction
The main components of wheat flour are starch and protein. Such flour is unique in having the property of forming a firm, elastic dough when mixed with water. This is made possible by the action of proteins which become hydrated and form an elastic complex called *gluten* when flour is kneaded with water. It is the presence of this elastic gluten that enables wheat flour to be converted into bread, though only types of wheat that produce a 'strong' flour containing more than 10% protein are suitable for bread-making. Flour made from cereals other than wheat (or rye which produces a weak gluten) cannot be used for making bread. Cornflour and ground rice, for example, contain only traces of protein and so cannot form gluten.

All types of flour have starch as the main component and cornflour, for example, is almost pure starch. Starch, which on examination under a microscope is found to consist of minute granules, will not dissolve in cold water. On heating a mixture of starch and water, the water diffuses through the walls of the granules and causes swelling. This begins at about 60°C and by $80\text{-}90^{\circ}$C the volume of the granules has increased fivefold and the starch is said to have *gelatinised*. The mixture is very thick and viscous and on cooling may set to from a solid clear *gel*. This explains the use of starch as a thickening agent and for making moulds and glazes.

When starch is used in cooking as a thickening agent, as for example in making pie fillings, other materials which may affect its setting properties are added. Sugar, for instance, has a marked effect because the sugar competes with the starch for the available water. This makes a proportion of the water unavailable to the starch and hinders gelatinisation. Acid substances, such as citric acid or lemon juice, have a similar effect in weakening the gel-forming properties of the starch.

The properties of gluten may also be modified when other materials are added to it. It has been found, for example, that gluten becomes stronger and more elastic if it is treated with a *flour improver.* Examples of flour improvers are ascorbic acid and potassium bromate and they are thought to act by an oxidation process in which proteins in the gluten become linked together to form longer protein chains of increased strength and elasticity. Salt is added to dough to improve its flavour, but it also affects the nature of the gluten by increasing its strength.

Required
Equipment:
250 cm^3 beakers
100 cm^3 beakers
glass rods
thermometers 0-110°C
waterbath
muslin cheese cloths
small basins or large beakers
oven — set at 250°C
sharp knife
Materials:
starches — maize, wheat, rice, potato, arrowroot etc.
flours — low protein cake flour
       high protein bread flour
       ordinary plain flour

Baked gluten balls from different flours.

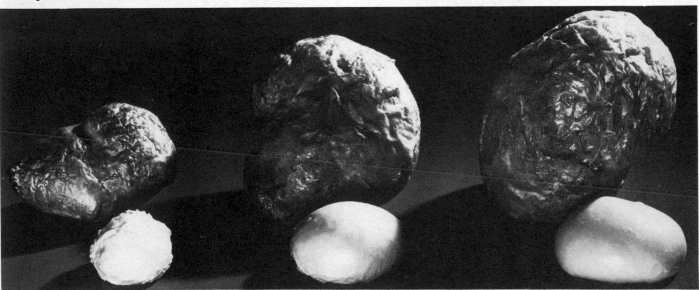

wholemeal
cornflour
ground rice
sugar
salt
lemon juice
ascorbic acid
potassium bromate

Method

1 Extraction of gluten from different flours

Weigh approx. 50 g of as many different flours as possible into separate small basins or beakers. Add sufficient cold water to each flour to mix it into a fairly stiff dough ball and knead well. Cover the dough ball with cold water and soak for about 15 mins.

Wash out the starch either by enclosing the dough ball in a fine mulsin cloth and kneading under cold running water until all the milky starch fluid has been removed — or by gently kneading the dough ball while still in the basin of water until most of the starch has been extracted and then finally kneading under the cold tap. Whichever method is used make sure that as much of the starch as possible is removed but that none of the gluten is lost.

Squeeze out as much water as possible and then weigh the wet gluten balls in order to compare the amount of gluten extracted from each flour. Also compare the elasticity and strength of each piece of gluten by pulling gently between the fingers.

Do any of the flours not produce gluten balls? Why is this? Which flour produces the most gluten; can you give a reason for this?

Remould the gluten balls into small even balls and then after labelling each one carefully, place all the gluten balls in a hot oven (250°C) for 20 mins. Remove from the oven, cool and then compare the changes in appearance.

Which gluten ball has swollen the most? Can you explain this?

Carefully cut each gluten ball in half with a sharp knife to examine the internal structure.

Which flour is most suitable for making bread? Why?

2 Effect of additives on gluten

Make up a series of 50 g dough balls from either strong bread flour or all purpose flour, with the following additives included in the mix:

a control, no addition
b 5 cm³ lemon juice
c 15 cm³ lemon juice
d 1 g salt
e 5 g salt
f 1 g ascorbic acid
g 1 g potassium bromate

Soak the dough balls in water for 15 mins. and then wash out the starch as before until just the gluten remains. Compare the colour, elasticity and strength of the wet gluten with the control sample and then bake all the balls in the oven (250°C for 20 mins.) and again compare them.

Do these additives have any effect on the gluten and if so where might they be of some use? What do you understand by the term flour improver? What flour improvers may be used in Great Britain?

3 Effect of heat on starch solutions

Place approx. 5 g of the various starches, wheat, maize, potato etc. in a 100 cm³ beaker and mix with 50 cm³ cold water.

Heat the beakers in a water bath to 100°C stirring continuously and observing any changes until all the solutions have thickened. Note the temperature at which each thickens. Allow to cool and then compare the thickness of the gel, the colour and the clarity.

Which starches would be most suitable for glazes and which for moulds? Why?

4 Effect of concentration on gelatinisation of starch

Weigh 3, 6, 9, 12, and 18 g of cornflour into separate 100 cm³ beakers and mix with 50 cm³ cold water. Add 2 g of sugar to each and slowly heat each solution stirring continuously until it thickens. Record the thickening temperature for each starch solution. Allow to cool and then compare the colour, texture and taste.

What is the danger of using too much cornflour as a thickening agent?

5 Effect of additives on gelatinisation of starch

For each sample weigh out 5 g of starch into a 100 cm³ beaker. Mix with 50 cm³ of cold water and make the following additions:

a control, no addition
b 0.5 g salt
c 3 g salt
d 10 g sugar
e 50 g sugar
f 10 cm³ lemon juice with 40 cm³ water
g 50 cm³ lemon juice — with no extra water

Heat each solution to 95°C stirring well as it thickens. Allow to cool and then compare the colour, clarity, thickness and taste with the control.

Which additives affect the gelatinisation? What application has this to products such as fruit pie fillings and lemon meringue pies?

13 Raising agents I–chemical

Scones are a typical example of a baked product in which baking powder is used as the raising agent.

Aims

1 To look for a single chemical substance that can be used successfully as a raising agent in cookery.
2 To investigate the properties of different acids which could be included in a baking powder.
3 To compare the rates of reaction of different baking powders.
4 To find the most suitable raising agent for making plain scones.

Introduction

Successful cooking often depends on producing a light open texture in the finished product; meringues, soufflés, bread, scones and sponge cakes are all typical examples of this. Such texture is created by the presence of steam, air or carbon dioxide gas. Steam is produced from water during cooking while air may be incorporated by mechanical mixing as when egg whites are whisked in making meringues (see unit 8). In many cases, especially when using recipes containing flour, carbon dioxide gas is used as the means of aeration.

Carbon dioxide may be produced by using a chemical *raising agent* or *baking powder*. The simplest type of raising agent is a single substance which breaks down on heating to produce carbon dioxide. Such substances usually have limitations, however, in baking. For example, sodium bicarbonate produces carbon dioxide on heating but breaks down to form sodium carbonate or 'washing soda' which if present in appreciable quantities may give the product an 'alkaline' or soapy taste and a yellow colour. A substance such as ammonium bicarbonate has the advantage that on heating it breaks down to form only gases (carbon dioxide, steam and ammonia) and so does not leave any solid residue behind in the baked goods.

For most purposes a baking powder is more suitable as a raising agent than a single substance. A baking powder is a mixture of substances which, when mixed with water and heated, produces carbon dioxide. It consists of 3 ingredients; sodium bicarbonate as the source of carbon dioxide, an acid or acid salt to liberate the gas from the bicarbonate and an inert filler, such as cornflour, to absorb moisture.

A variety of different acid substances may be used in a baking powder. The aim is to use one which does not react with cold water (or much of the gas would be lost before baking started) but which does produce a good volume of gas on heating and which leaves only a white, tasteless, harmless solid residue in the baked product. Baking powder may be classed as fast, medium, or slow according to the rate at which gas is produced on heating. A simple way of measuring the gas produced from a baking powder is to add enough egg white to the water to hold the gas bubbles produced. The volume of egg white foam is then a measure of the volume of gas formed.

Required

Equipment:
oven set at 230°C
test tubes
250 cm^3 measuring cylinders
400 cm^3 beaker
mixing bowls
pastry boards
rolling pins
sharp knives
pastry cutters (if available)

Materials:
Litmus paper
universal indicator solution
sodium bicarbonate
sodium carbonate
ammonium bicarbonate
vinegar
tartaric acid
cream of tartar
lime water
calcium hydrogen phosphate (acid calcium phosphate ACP)
Disodium dihydrogen pyrophosphate (acid sodium pyrophosphate, ASP)
glucono delta lactone (GDL)
selection of commercial baking powders, including some American ones if possible
1 egg
1000 g plain flour
250 g margarine
1½ pints milk
salt

Method

1 Single substance raising agent

Test the effectiveness of the 3 chemicals indicated as follows:

a Put approx. 2 g sodium bicarbonate into each of 2 dry test tubes. To one tube add cold water and to the other boiling water (approx. 5 cm^3) and observe what happens. Reheat both tubes noticing any further reaction. Test some of the gas coming off by passing it into dilute lime water. When the reaction has subsided, shake the tubes well and then taste the residue before testing the solution with litmus paper.
Add vinegar drops to both tubes until there is no further reaction and again test with litmus paper.

b Repeat with sodium carbonate.

c Repeat with ammonium bicarbonate.

What does part a tell you about the value of sodium bicarbonate as a raising agent? Why was there a further reaction when vinegar was added? What are the disadvantages of using sodium carbonate or ammonium bicarbonate as raising agents?

2 Nature of acid ingredients

a For each of the following acid ingredients, put 2 g into each of 2 dry test tubes and add cold water to one and boiling water to the other. Shake well and notice whether they dissolve and if there is any effervescence. Add a few drops of vinegar to each tube and again look for any effervescence.

  (i) tartaric acid
 (ii) cream of tartar
(iii) acid calcium phosphate (ACP)
(iv) acid sodium pyrophosphate (ASP)
 (v) glucono delta lactone (GDL)

Could any of these substances be used as a single substance raising agent? Why? What effect will the solubility of the acid ingredient have on the speed of reaction when it is mixed with sodium bicarbonate in a baking powder?

b Put approx. 2 g sodium bicarbonate into 5 dry test tubes, add the specified amount of acid ingredient. Add 5 cm^3 cold water and shake. Observe any reaction and then gently heat each tube noting the speed of effervescence i.e. the rate at which bubbles are produced.

  (i) 2 g tartaric acid
 (ii) 4 g cream of tartar
(iii) 2.5 g acid calcium phosphate
(iv) 2.5 g acid sodium pyrophosphate
 (v) 4 g glucono delta lactone

Which of these acid ingredients produces a fast acting baking powder and which a slow acting one?

3 Rates of reaction of baking powders

a Using as wide a variety of commerical baking powders as possible, put a small amount into a test tube, add cold water and shake well before gently heating. Try and decide which of these baking powders are fast acting and which slow and then try and guess what their constituents might be. Where possible this can be checked by looking at the ingredient list on the packet.

Why do commercial baking powders often include cornflour or other neutral ingredients?

The use of different amounts of baking powder in a cake showing the effect of excess (centre), none (right) compared with the correct amount (left).

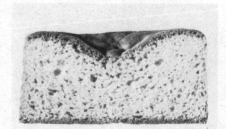

b Mix the white of an egg with 200 cm³ cold water. Put 5 g of a wide variety of commerical baking powders into the bottom of several 250 cm³ measuring cylinders, add 25 cm³ egg white solution and invert twice to mix. Leave to stand and record the volume of foam reached after 10 mins.

Which baking powder produces the greatest volume of foam in the time? How is this related to your decision in **a** as to which were fast acting and which slow acting baking powders?

These experiments could be repeated with the students using their own formulated baking powders using acids from experiment **2** in order to get fast, medium and slow acting baking powders.

4 Experimental scone baking

Basic recipe: 100 g plain flour
25 g margarine
pinch salt
60 cm³ milk

Sift flour and salt together and rub in the fat. Add the milk and knead into a light spongy dough. Roll out to approx. 1 cm thick on a floured board. Cut into 6 equally sized pieces (using all the mixture) either with a pastry cutter or by cutting triangles. Place 3 scones in the oven (230°C) immediately and cook for approx. 10 mins., leaving the other 3 in a warm atmosphere for 30 mins. before cooking in the same way.

Make up 9 batches of scones, modifying the basic recipe by adding the following raising agents to the flour:

a Control — no addition

b ½ tsp sodium bicarbonate

c 1 tsp sodium bicarbonate

d ½ tsp sodium bicarbonate + ½ tsp tartaric acid

e ½ tsp sodium bicarbonate + 1 tsp cream of tartar

f ½ tsp sodium bicarbonate + 1 tsp glucono delta lactone

g 1 tsp commercial baking powder

h 2 tsp commercial baking powder

i use self raising flour instead of plain flour

When the scones are cool compare the increase in volume with reference to the control and notice any other difference in external appearance. Slice the scones in half and compare the texture and the colour.

Two methods of washing starch out of a dough (experiment 1 unit 12).

Pour a few drops of universal indicator solution onto the cut surface of each scone and record the pH. This can also be used to show whether the baking powder and the flour were well mixed at the beginning.

How is the pH related to the colour of the scone?

Finally taste the scones and compare their flavour and texture. Which scones are the most acceptable? Is there any difference between the scones cooked immediately and those left for 30 minutes? If so, for which modification is this the most noticeable?

What has caused the unusual colour and flavour of the scones made with sodium bicarbonate alone? Which common substance could have been used along with the sodium bicarbonate to overcome these changes if none of the acid salts were available?

If necessary further modifications to the recipe could be carried out to find the optimum amount of baking powder to be used or to test the students own formulated baking powders from experiment **3**.

Follow up
Glucono delta lactone (GDL) is not itself an acid but at low temperatures it very slowly reacts with water to produce an acid called *gluconic acid*. This acid reacts at high temperatures to produce carbon dioxide. Find out as much as you can about the use of GDL in frozen doughs, and explain why it is preferred in such cases to the more common acid ingredients of baking powders.

14 Raising agents II–biological

Aims

1 To investigate the fermentation action of yeast and how it is affected by various additives.
2 To investigate the effect of temperature on the fermentation rate.
3 To look at the effect of recipe variation on the fermentation of bread dough.

Introduction

Whereas a *chemical* raising agent is used in making cakes (see unit 13), a *biological* raising agent is used in making bread. Bread is aerated by carbon dioxide gas produced by a fermentation process which is brought about by the action of enzymes present in yeast. Yeast consists of tiny cells too small to be seen except through a microscope. When yeast is incorporated in dough the yeast cells live and multiply by using the nutrients of the dough as food. Enzymes in the yeast break down sugars present in the dough (and any added sugar) producing carbon dioxide and alcohol.

The enzymes in yeast, being proteins, are very sensitive to conditions, for example, temperature. The enzymes in yeast are most active at 25-35°C and above 35°C their activity decreases until at 55-60°C the yeast cells are killed and enzyme activity ceases. Fresh yeast may be stored successfully by freezing it, because this inactivates the enzymes without killing the yeast. Enzyme activity is affected by the presence of other substances and, for example, is increased by addition of sugar but decreased by addition of salt.

The essential ingredients in making bread are flour, yeast, water and salt. The essence of breadmaking is to form a dough from the flour and water (see unit 12) that is springy and elastic. During *proving* the dough is kept warm so that fermentation, with consequent aeration of the dough, is encouraged. The salt not only influences the rate of fermentation but also strengthens and toughens the gluten and improves flavour. Apart from the four essential ingredients in bread, a number of others may also be used. Sugar, for example, may be added and has the effect of speeding up fermentation, producing a brown crust and improving flavour. In making milk bread, milk is added to improve flavour and make the crust browner. Fat is sometimes added to bread because it increases the tenderness of both crust and crumb as well as improving flavour. Oxidising agents such as ascorbic acid may also be added because of their action as flour improvers (unit 12).

Once the dough is sufficiently strong, springy and elastic it is baked in a hot oven for 30-50 minutes. At first enzyme action continues and the dough rises. Subsequently as the temperature increases, yeast cells die and enzyme activity ceases, starch grains swell and gelatinize and gluten coagulates giving firmness to the structure.

Required

Equipment:
large oven, set at 225°C
test tubes
sharp knives
mixing bowls
bunsen burner and tripod or gas ring
small pan or large beaker
1 lb loaf tins
100 cm³ beakers
250 cm³ beakers
pastry board
Materials:
200 g compressed fresh yeast
4 g dried yeast
100 g sugar
100 g salt
lard
4000 g bread flour
250 g cake flour
150 g wholemeal flour
250 g self raising flour
25 g cornflour
ascorbic acid

Method

1 Fermentation action of yeast

Weigh 8 samples of approx. 4 g compressed fresh yeast into small beakers with the additions mentioned below:

a 20 cm³ cold water

b 20 cm³ cold water + ½ tsp sugar

c 20 cm³ lukewarm water

d 20 cm³ lukewarm water + ½ tsp sugar

e 20 cm³ lukewarm water + 2 tsp bread flour

f 20 cm³ lukewarm water + 2 tsp cornflour

g 20 cm³ lukewarm water + ½ tsp salt

h 20 cm³ boiling water + ½ tsp. sugar

Keep beakers (a) and (b) cold and beakers (d) to (h) warm (approx. 35°C) for 30 mins. before looking at them to see if there is any fermentation shown by production of gas bubbles.

Which is the best temperature for action of yeast?
Does sugar make any difference to fermentation rate?
Does salt have any effect?
Can you explain the effect of the two types of flour?

2 Effect of temperature on the rate of fermentation

a Mix 4 g compressed yeast with 20 cm³ lukewarm water and add to 30 g warm bread flour. Knead into a smooth

dough and divide into 3 equal portions:
(i) Bake in a hot oven at 225°C for 10 mins.
(ii) Keep cool for 30 mins. and bake in a hot oven for 10 mins.
(iii) Keep warm for 30 mins. and bake in a hot oven for 10 mins.

b Repeat **a** using very cold water and very cold flour.

c Repeat **a** using boiling water and very hot flour.

Cool the rolls and compare their volumes. Explain the differences in size and decide which is the most suitable temperature for the water and flour and the best baking procedure.
This simple method could be extended to look at the effect of oven temperature on other ingredients.

3 Experimental bread baking
Basic recipe: 250 g bread flour
1 tsp salt
1 tsp sugar
7 g yeast (compressed)
150 cm³ warm water

Crumble the yeast into a 250 cm³ beaker and mix with the sugar and warm water.
Sift the flour and salt together and pour the yeast mixture into the centre. Mix into a smooth dough and knead for 10 mins. on a floured board.
Leave to prove for 30 mins. in a warm place and then knock back the dough to redistribute the yeast. Place in greased loaf tins and leave to prove for a further 30 mins. until well risen.
Bake in a hot oven at 225°C for approx. 40 mins.
Make up batches of bread modifying the basic recipe as indicated:

a *Effect of salt on dough*
Make 3 loaves containing:
(i) none
(ii) 1 tsp salt
(iii) 3 tsp salt

b *Effect of sugar on dough*
Make 3 loaves containing:
(i) none
(ii) 1 tsp sugar
(iii) 3 tsp sugar

c *Effect of yeast on dough*
Make 4 loaves containing:
(i) none
(ii) 7 g yeast
(iii) 50 g yeast
(iv) 4 g dried yeast

d *Effect of flour on dough*
Make 4 loaves using:
(i) bread flour
(ii) cake flour
(iii) wholemeal flour
(iv) self raising flour

e *Effect of other additives*
Make 4 loaves containing:
(i) basic recipe

(ii) 150 cm³ warm milk instead of water
(iii) basic recipe plus 25 g lard
(iv) basic recipe plus 3 g ascorbic acid

Each set contains a loaf of the basic recipe for standardisation. Cool all the loaves and within each set compare the shape, volume and colour of the crust before cutting the loaf in half and comparing the colour, texture and taste of the crumb.

Can you explain the effect of salt and sugar on the bread dough?
Does it matter whether fresh or dried yeast is used?
What is the effect of using cake flour or wholemeal flour on the loaf structure?
Is it any advantage to use self raising flour?
How does the addition of milk and fat affect the crumb structure?
What role does ascorbic acid play in the recipe?

Follow up
Bread is one of our most important foods and the nature of the breadmaking process has only been touched on briefly in the introduction. Find out as much as you can about:
1 different types of flour used for breadmaking
2 the importance in the breadmaking process of enzymes present in yeast and flour
3 different ways in which bread is made commercially.
You can find information in;
The Experimental Study of Foods by Griswold chapters 9 and 11
Food Science — a chemical approach by Fox and Cameron chapter 8

A selection of different types of bread emphasising the wide range available. How many do you recognise?

15 Flour cookery–the role of ingredients

Aims

1 To investigate the effect of ingredient variation in a basic Victoria Sandwich cake.
2 To find the best flour for making plain biscuits.

Introduction

In making a cake which is shortened by fat as discussed in this unit, it is important to understand the functions of the main ingredients; fat, flour, sugar, eggs and baking powder. A cake recipe is chosen to give a balance between ingredients that contribute to *volume* and those that contribute to *structure.* If ingredients contributing to volume are present in too small a proportion, the cake does not rise properly during baking and the product has a close heavy texture. On the other hand if they are present in too large a proportion, the cake at first rises rapidly during baking but later sinks.

In a rich cake such as a Victoria Sandwich the basic recipe contains equal weights of fat, self raising flour, sugar and eggs together with a little milk if desired. In such a recipe egg white, fat and baking powder contribute to volume while flour and eggs contribute to structure. Sugar improves texture and flavour. In making such a cake, fat is warmed to increase its plasticity and then creamed with sugar by beating the two together so entrapping air which assists the action of baking powder in aerating the cake during baking. Eggs are beaten to incorporate air, and after being added to the creamed mixture beating is continued until the mix is light and foamy.

The resulting mixture is an aerated emulsion stabilized by *lecithin* in the egg yolk. After folding in the self raising flour the aerated mix is baked. During baking the air bubbles expand and the film which surrounds them becomes stronger as adsorbed proteins in egg white coagulate. The structure of the cake becomes stronger as proteins of the flour and eggs coagulate and at the same time starch from the flour gelatinizes producing a strong network of protein in which starch is embedded.

Both the quality as well as the quantity of ingredients are important in cake making. For example, the nature of flour used affects the texture of the cake and the most suitable type of flour is one which has a low protein content (i.e. a weak flour) and a fine texture (i.e. small particle size). Strong flour such as is used for making bread (unit 14) or coarse flour such as wholemeal do not produce high quality cakes.

The type of flour used is also important in making biscuits as it affects the texture of the final product. For example, a coarse flour such as wholemeal produces a coarse texture such as is required in wholemeal or 'digestive' type biscuits. A weak flour is used to produce biscuits having a soft, tender crumb whereas a stong flour produces a better developed gluten and hence biscuits of larger volume which also have a less tender texture than those produced from soft flour. Self raising flour may be used for making biscuits of the 'water biscuit' or 'cracker' type where a well aerated flaky texture is desired.

Required

Equipment:
mixing bowls
wooden spoons
cake tins and paper cases
egg whisks/beaters
oven set at 180°C
rolling pin
pastry board
pastry cutters
baking sheets

Materials:
1000 g self raising flour
100 g plain cake flour
100 g bread flour
100 g cornflour
100 g wholemeal flour
50 g arrowroot
1500 g caster sugar
1500 g margarine
26 eggs
salt
¼ pint milk
baking powder

*The use of different amounts of sugar in a cake (see **1 e**) showing the effect of too little (right), too much (centre), compared with the control (left).*

Method

1 Experimental cake making

Basic recipe: 50 g margarine
50 g caster sugar
50 g self raising flour
1 egg

Cream fat and sugar together until light and creamy. Add beaten egg gradually and beat well. Fold in the flour and place mixture in 16-18 cm paper case inside cake tin. Bake for approx. 30 mins at 180°C.

Make batches of cakes as indicated below, modifying the basic recipe by altering one ingredient at a time:

a *Quantity of self raising flour*
Make 3 cakes containing:
(i) 25 g flour
(ii) 50 g flour
(iii) 75 g flour

b *Type of flour*
Make 4 cakes containing:
(i) 50 g cake flour
(ii) 50 g bread flour
(iii) 50 g cornflour
(iv) 50 g wholemeal flour,
including ½ tsp baking powder for each of these.

c *Type of raising agent*
Make 4 cakes containing:
(i) 50 g cake flour
(ii) 50 g cake flour + ½ tsp baking powder
(iii) 50 g self raising flour
(iv) 50 g self raising flour + ½ tsp baking powder

d *Quantity of fat*
Make 3 cakes containing:
(i) 10 g fat
(ii) 50 g fat
(iii) 100 g fat

e *Quantity of sugar*
Make 3 cakes containing:
(i) 10 g sugar
(ii) 50 g sugar
(iii) 100 g sugar

f *Quantity of egg*
Make 3 cakes containing:
(i) none
(i) 1 egg
(iii) 2 eggs

g *Added liquid*
Make 3 cakes containing
(i) none
(ii) 10 cm³ milk
(iii) 50 cm³ milk

Most of the modifications include one cake baked to the basic recipe to help with comparisons and standardisation.

When all the cakes are cool, within each set compare the external shape, colour, volume and general appearance before cutting in half to examine the colour, texture, degree of aeration and taste.

Explain the reasons for these variations in the finished cakes.

Do you think that the basic recipe is the best which could be used? If not, suggest suitable modifications.

2 Flour in biscuits

Basic recipe 50 g flour
25 g caster sugar
25 g margarine
pinch salt
15 g beaten egg

Mix flour and sugar in a bowl and rub in the fat until the mixture resembles fine bread crumbs. Add beaten egg and mix to a stiff paste.

Roll out thinly on a floured board and cut into about 10 biscuits.

Bake on greased baking sheets for 15 mins. at 180°C.

Make 6 sets of biscuits as above but using different flours making sure that all the biscuits are cut to the same size and shape:

a cake flour

b bread flour

c wholemeal flour

d self raising flour

e arrowroot

f cornflour

Cool all the biscuits and compare their appearance, colour texture, size, shape and taste.

Which flour makes the best biscuits? How do you account for this?

Further modifications can be done with this recipe to look at the effect of varying the amounts of flour, sugar and fat as in the cake method.

Follow up

Find out as much as you can about the functions of fat in a cake mixture and how the proportion of fat in the recipe affects the nature of the baked cake. What are the best sorts of fat for use in making cakes? Give your reasons. Find out what is meant by the term *high ratio* or *super glycerinated* fat and the advantage of using such a fat in commercial cake manufacture.

16 Fruit and vegetables I–colour

Aims

1 To investigate the different pigments present in fruit and vegetables.
2 To study the effect on these pigments of various cooking procedures.

Introduction

The colour of fruit and vegetables is one of their most attractive properties and one of the principle aims in cooking them is to preserve the colour of the fresh product as far as is possible. We have already seen (units 1 and 2) how the nature of water used in cooking vegetables — whether it is hard or soft or acid or alkaline — affects the result, including the final colour. In this unit the aim is to investigate in more detail how individual pigments in fruit and vegetables are affected by cooking.

The main factors which affect the colour of cooked fruit and vegetables are:

a cooking temperature

b cooking time

c pH

d presence of metals.

The predominant green colour of leafy plants is due to the presence of *chlorophyll*. Chlorophyll exists in 2 forms, one of which is blue-black and the other blue-green. These forms are always accompanied by the yellow *carotenoids* and the colour of green vegetables such as lettuce and cabbage results from a combination of all three.

Chlorophyll is affected by pH and its colour changes to olive green in acid conditions due to the formation of *pheophytin* and to bright green in alkali due to the formation of *chlorophyllin*. Chlorophyll is sensitive to the presence of metals such as iron or copper which both produce a bright green colour; note, however, that the latter is toxic except in trace amounts.

Carotenoids are responsible for the yellow and orange colour of fruit and vegetables such as carrots (hence the name), tomatoes and peaches. They are hardly affected by temperature, cooking time or changes of pH. On the other hand they are affected by oxidation in air which results in loss of colour as is seen, for example, in dried carrots.

Anthocyanins are responsible for the red-blue colour of fruits and vegetables such as plums and red cabbage. They are sensitive to pH being purple in neutral conditions, red in acid and blue in alkali. They are stable to heat but because they are very soluble in water they may be bleached out of vegetables during cooking leaving them pale in colour.

Anthoxanthins are closely related to anthocyanins and are colourless or yellow in colour. They occur, for example, in potatoes and some onions. They are sensitive to pH and in alkali turn yellow or orange.

Tannins are best known for the astringent flavour they impart to tea, but they also affect the flavour as well as the colour of fruit and vegetables such as apples, pears and peaches. Although tannins are usually colourless they oxidise to give a brown colour when fruit such as peaches are sliced; they are also sensitive to pH and darken in alkali.

Required

Equipment:
500 cm^3 beakers or small pans
sharp vegetable knives
bunsen burners or gas rings
100 cm^3 beakers
250 cm^3 beakers
chinagraph pencils or gummed labels
glass rods and teaspoons
universal indicator pH paper

Materials:
500 g brussels sprouts
500 g dark green leafy vegetable — e.g. spinach, cabbage
500 g red cabbage
500 g beetroot
250 g onions
500 g carrots
250 g cauliflower
3 pears
white vinegar
sodium bicarbonate
5% ferrous sulphate solution
salt
lemon juice
dilute hydrochloric acid

Method

1 Chlorophyll

Take 500 g leafy green vegetable, wash well and shred finely. Weigh out 8 samples of approx. 50 g each and plunge into a small pan or 500 cm^3 beaker containing 100 cm^3 boiling water. Each pan should be clearly labelled and the following additions made before the vegetables are added:

a no addition — control sample

b ¼ tsp salt

c 1.0 cm^3 vinegar

d 10 cm^3 dilute acid (e.g. hydrochloric acid)

e pinch sodium bicarbonate

f ½ teaspoon sodium bicarbonate

g 5 cm^3 iron solution (e.g. ferrous sulphate)

h no addition

Simmer samples a to g for 10 mins. and then drain the

What colour is 'red' cabbage when it is raw (left), cooked in hard water (centre) and pickled (right)?

water from each into separate clearly labelled small beakers. Transfer the cooked vegetables to clean clearly labelled larger beakers. For sample **h**, plunge the vegetable into the boiling water and immediately remove. Again retain both water and vegetable.

Observe the colour and measure of pH of the different waters.

Observe the colour and texture of the cooked vegetables. Repeat the experiment using small whole brussels sprouts.

Acids are present in green vegetables and are released on cooking. Some of these acids are volatile and so are lost in the steam when vegetables are cooked without a cover. Why may the colour of green vegetables be better if they are cooked in a pan without a cover?

2 Carotenoids
Repeat experiment **1** using samples of carrots simmering each for 15 mins. before draining.

3 Anthocyanins
Take 500 g of firm red cabbage, wash well and shred finely. Prepare 8 samples and treat as in experiment **1** simmering each for 10 mins.
After reporting on the colour, texture and pH of the cabbage, take the cooking water from **d** and **f** and perform the following experiments;

(i) Add a small amount of sodium bicarbonate to water **d** observing any colour changes. Continue adding sodium bicarbonate until a constant colour is achieved.

(ii) Add a few drops of vinegar to water **f** observing any colour changes. Continue until a constant colour is achieved.

What does this tell you about these colour changes? Repeat the above using small cubes of beetroot.

Red fruits cooked in aluminium pans often turn bluish. Would you have expected this from your observations in this experiment?

4 Anthoxanthins
Peel and roughly chop the onions. Weigh out 8 samples of 50 g and treat as in experiment **1** simmering each for 15 mins. before observing the colour, texture and pH. Repeat the above using small pieces of cauliflower.

What could you add to the cooking water when boiling onions to ensure that they stay white?

5 Tannins
Peel, quarter and core 3 pears and stew for 30 mins. in pans containing 500 cm³ water with the following additions:

a no addition — control sample

b 20 cm³ lemon juice

c 1 teaspoon sodium bicarbonate

Drain the remaining liquid into small glass beakers and transfer the pears into larger beakers — all clearly labelled. Compare the colour and texture of the pears and the colour and pH of the cooking waters.

Conclusions
1 For each of the above experiments:

a Is the pigment soluble in water?

b How is the pigment affected by acid conditions?

c How is the pigment affected by alkali conditions?

d How is the pigment affected by the presence of iron?

2 From the results of experiments **3** and **4** can you account for the rather unexpected colour of the red cabbage cooked in excess sodium bicarbonate?

3 What recommendations would you make as to the best methods of cooking these different vegetables in order to retain the desired colour?

Question
Very old recipe books contain some strange recipes of which the following for improving the green colour of green vegetables preserved in vinegar is typical.
'To render pickles green, boil them with halfpence, or allow them to stand for 24 hours in copper or brass pans'. Do you think the method would be successful? Comment on the health aspect of the method. Can you suggest a better way of achieving a similar result?

17 Fruit and vegetables II – vitamin C content

A selection of fruit and vegetables (see Follow up).

Aims
1 To measure the Vitamin C content of fresh fruit and vegetables.
2 To compare the amount of Vitamin C lost from vegetables prepared in different ways.

Introduction
From a nutritional point of view fruit and vegetables are important because they supply us with most (nearly 90% in Britain) of our intake of *Vitamin C (ascorbic acid).* Of all the vitamins ascorbic acid is the only one that can be measured easily and this can be done by using a simple *titration* technique (see unit 2), although the method cannot be applied to highly coloured foods.

Vitamin C is easily destroyed by oxidation especially at high temperatures and for this reason much of the Vitamin C in food may be destroyed by cooking. The fact that ascorbic acid is easily oxidised is the basis of its determination in food. A blue dye, known by the formidable name *2:6 dichlorophenol indophenol,* is reduced to a colourless form by ascorbic acid. Thus if the blue dye is placed in a burette and titrated against the food (liquidized first if solid) containing ascorbic acid the dye is decolourized. The dye indicator solution is added until it has reacted with all the ascorbic acid present. This point – the end point of titration – is reached when a faint pink colour persists for 10 seconds. The pink colour is explained by the fact that at the end point a small excess (about 1 drop) of dye is present, and that the dye is pink in the presence of acid.

In order to calculate the amount of Vitamin C present in food it is necessary to *standardize* the dye solution, i.e. find out its strength in terms of the amount of Vitamin C equivalent to 1 cm^3 of indicator solution. This can be done by titrating the dye with a solution containing a known amount of ascorbic acid. This is described in experiment **1(c)**.

The ease with which Vitamin C is destroyed has already been mentioned and has many important consequences. For example, the amount of Vitamin C in fruit and vegetables decreases due to oxidation when they are stored. For this reason old potatoes may have less than half the Vitamin C content of new potatoes. Loss of Vitamin C occurs when fruit and vegetables are cooked, and the higher the temperature and the longer the cooking time the greater is the amount of the vitamin lost. In addition the oxygen present in cooking water (in conjunction with enzymes – oxidases – in the fruit or vegetable) causes destruction of Vitamin C and for this reason it is best to put vegetables directly in boiling water (which contains no dissolved oxygen and which rapidly destroys enzymes) rather than into cold water which is then brought to the boil. Vitamin C is soluble in water and for this reason it is desirable to limit the quantity of water used for cooking to reduce the amount of Vitamin C lost by solution into the water.

Required

Equipment:
100 cm^3 measuring cylinder
50 cm^3 burettes
5 cm^3 pipettes
10 cm^3 pipettes
20 cm^3 pipettes
100 cm^3 graduated flasks
2000 cm^3 graduated flask
250 cm^3 graduated flask
100 cm^3 conical flasks
250 cm^3 measuring cylinders
muslin cloths
lemon squeezer
sharp vegetable knives
liquidizer
small pans or large beakers
gas rings or bunsen burners

Materials:
ascorbic acid
2:6 dichlorophenol indophenol
metaphosphoric acid — made up in 20% solution
1 lemon
1 orange
1 large dark green cabbage (e.g. spring cabbage)
1 large pale green cabbage
500 g brussels sprouts

Method

1 Preparation and standardisation of solutions

a *Preparation of indicator solution.* Weigh out 0.4 g of 2:6 dichlorophenol indophenol, dissolve in water and make up to 2000 cm^3 in a graduated flask (concentration is 0.2mg/cm^3).
This dye is bright blue in alkaline solution and pink in acid. When it reacts with ascorbic acid it is decolourized.

b *Preparation of standard ascorbic acid solution.* Weigh out 0.05 g pure ascorbic acid, dissolve in 60 cm^3 of 20% metaphophoric acid and make up to 250 cm^3 with water in a graduated flask (concentration is 0.2mg/cm^3). The metaphosphoric acid is added to prevent oxidation of the ascorbic acid.
Both solutions are rather unstable and should be made up just before they are required and stored in a refrigerator.

c *Standardisation of dye solution.* Rinse the burette with some of the blue dye solution and then fill to the zero mark. Pipette exactly 5 cm^3 of ascorbic acid solution into a conical flask and run in the blue dye until the faint pink colour remains for 10 secs. Repeat the titration until consistent results are achieved.

Why is the end point of the titration when the pink colour appears?

Calculation
5 cm^3 ascorbic acid solution contain 5 x 0.2 = 1 mg
If x cm^3 of blue dye were required
x cm^3 of blue dye is equivalent to 1 mg ascorbic acid
1 cm^3 of blue dye is equivalent to $\frac{1}{x}$ mg ascorbic acid.

For all the following experiments, every cm^3 of blue dye used is equivalent to 1/x mg Vitamin C in the sample.

2 Vitamin C in citrus fruits

Extract the juice from a fresh lemon and filter carefully to remove any pips or other solid matter. Pipette 20 cm^3 juice into a 100 cm^3 graduated flask, and 10 cm^3 20% metaphosphoric acid and make up to the mark with water. Shake well and then pipette exactly 10 cm^3 diluted juice into a conical flask and titrate with blue dye as above. Repeat with further samples of diluted juice until the burette readings are constant.

Calculation
If y cm^3 blue dye are required, this is equivalent to y/x mg of Vitamin C.
Each 10 cm^3 sample of diluted juice contains 2 cm^3 pure lemon juice
∴ 2 cm^3 pure lemon juice contains y/x mg Vitamin C and 100 cm^3 pure lemon juice contains 50 y/x mg Vitamin C.
Hence the amount of Vitamin C in lemon juice can be calculated.

Repeat this using the juice of a fresh orange. Compare your results with those in recognised Food Composition Tables. If using a liquidizer the Vitamin C content of a whole lemon or orange can be calculated rather than juice only. If possible repeat the experiment using other citrus fruits to compare Vitamin C content or using oranges which have been stored for several weeks to see if there is any loss of Vitamin C on storage.

3 Distribution of Vitamin C in cabbage leaves

Carefully separate the leaves from a pale green cabbage and weigh out three 50 g samples from:
(i) outermost darkest leaves
(ii) innermost white heart of cabbage
(iii) pale green leaves from middle portion.
To each sample add 50 cm^3 20% metaphosphoric acid and 150 cm^3 water and liquidize. Add to a 250 cm^3 measuring cylinder and make up to the 250 cm^3 mark by adding water. Strain the liquid through muslin to remove any remaining solid matter. Pipette 10 cm^3 of this liquid into a conical flask and titrate with blue dye as before. Repeat until constant readings are achieved.

Calculation
If z cm^3 blue dye are required, this is equivalent to z/x mg Vitamin C.
Total volume of 250 cm^3 liquid contains 50 g cabbage
∴ 10 cm^3 liquid contains 2 g cabbage
∴ 2 g cabbage contains z/x mg Vitamin C
Hence the amount of Vitamin C in 100 g cabbage can be calculated.

Where is most of the Vitamin C in a cabbage to be found?

From the remaining cabbage leaves take a random 50 g sample and repeat the procedure above in order to get an average result for Vitamin C content of raw cabbage.

4   Vitamin C content of other vegetables
Repeat the process from experiment **3** to determine the Vitamin C content of dark green spring cabbage, Brussels sprouts and other vegetables. Compare your results with those quoted in recognised Food Composition Tables.

5   Effect of cooking on Vitamin C loss
Use either cabbage or sprouts to determine the effect that different cooking times and additives have on the Vitamin C content.
Carefully weigh out six equivalent 50 g samples of the raw vegetables and treat as follows:

a   Add 50 cm^3 20% metaphosphoric acid, 150 cm^3 water and liquidize. Continue as in experiment **3** to obtain a value for the raw vegetable.

b   Place in 200 cm^3 cold water and boil for 10 mins. Strain the vegetables, add 50 cm^3 20 % metaphosphoric acid, 150 cm^3 water and liquidize. Continue as before.

c   as in **b** but boil for 20 mins.

d   as in **b** but boil for 30 mins.

e   as in **b** but include ½ teaspoon of salt and boil for 20 mins.

f   as in **b** but include ½ teaspoon of sodium bicarbonate and boil for 20 mins.

Other modifications of times and additives can be tried from these results. Work out an approx. % loss of Vitamin C for each method of cooking.

What is the effect of boiling the vegetables for a long time?
Does the addition of (i) salt (ii) sodium bicarbonate have any effect on the % Vitamin C lost during cooking?

Questions

Blackcurrant juice is a good source of Vitamin C. Why cannot the simple method of ascorbic acid determination described in this unit be used in this case?
Why does the ascorbic acid content of vegetables and fruit decrease when they are stored?
Why is it that when a standard solution of ascorbic acid is prepared it is made (i) just before it is required and (ii) with the addition of metaphosphoric acid?
Why is it desirable to eat vegetables immediately after they have been cooked, rather than keeping them hot for some time before they are eaten?

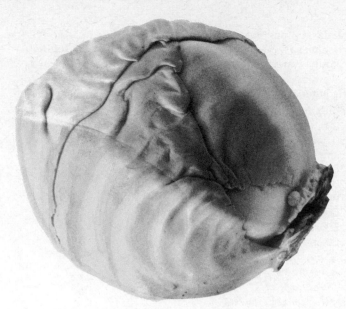

From the results of this unit would you say that cabbage is a rich source of Vitamin C? Which part of the cabbage is richest in Vitamin C?

Follow up

1 Prepare a chart entitled 'How to reduce loss of Vitamin C when vegetables are cooked'. In the first column list the precautions to be taken and in the second column give a brief explanation of each precaution suggested.

2 Identify from the photograph as many fruit and vegetables as you can. Check their Vitamin C content in Food Composition Tables and list them in order of Vitamin C present. Using the table below comment on the difference between the content of Vitamin C present and the contribution made in the diet. Why may these two be so different? From the values given in the table would you say that fruit are important sources of Vitamin A, calcium and iron?

	The importance of fruit and vegetables in the diet			
	% contribution to the diet			
	Vitamin A	Vitamin C	Calcium	Iron
Vegetables				
Potatoes	–	25	1	9
Cabbage, sprouts and cauliflower	1	9	1	2
Leafy salads	1	2	–	–
Legumes (peas, beans)	1	2	–	1
Tomatoes	1	6	–	1
Carrots	15	1	1	1
All vegetables	**23**	**54**	**6**	**22**
Fruit				
Oranges	–	10	–	–
Lemons, grapefruit	–	2	–	–
Apples, pears	–	2	–	1
Soft fruit (e.g. raspberries)	–	3	–	–
Bananas	–	1	–	–
All fruit	**1**	**32**	**2**	**4**

18 Fruit and vegetables III—cooking methods

Aims
1 To discover the best method of cooking various vegetables in order to achieve a good flavour, texture and colour and the retention of maximum Vitamin C.

2 To discover the best method of preparing apple purée.

Introduction
In units 16 and 17 the colour, vitamin C content and, to some extent, the texture of vegetables have been investigated. We now turn to the important aspect of flavour.

Vegetables and fruits have very delicate characteristic flavours resulting from the presence of a large number of substances, often present in only trace amounts. Some of the most important of these substances are volatile, ie. they have a high vapour pressure and easily vaporize on heating; such substances are partly lost either by vaporizing or by dissolving in the cooking water when fruit and vegetables are cooked. In addition some volatile substances are often produced by the cooking process. Non-volatile substances are also important as flavours and cooking affects them either because they are soluble in water and therefore dissolve in the cooking water, or because they break down on heating.

The flavour of fruit is characterised as being both sharp and sweet, and although these characteristics are less obvious in vegetables, both fruit and vegetables contain acids and sugars as important flavour constituents. For example, *glucose* is found in grapes and many other sweet fruits and also, more surprisingly, the substantial amounts in onions and unripe potatoes. Examples of acids are *malic* and *citric* acids which are two of the commonest acids found in fruits, and *oxalic* acid which occurs in both fruits and vegetables, particularly spinach and rhubarb.

Sulphur-containing compounds are important in vegetables, particularly in those of the cabbage and onion families. For example, when cabbage is cooked the volatile sulphur compounds *dimethyl sulphide* and *hydrogen sulphide* are formed. Overcooking of cabbage increases the amount of sulphur-volatile compounds formed and contributes to the rather unpleasant taste and small of overcooked cabbage. Hydrogen sulphide is also one of the sulphur compounds formed when onions are cooked, but unlike cabbage, boiled onions become milder in flavour on cooking because the volatile sulphur compounds are lost either as vapour or in the cooking water.

Investigation of volatile substances
The apparatus used in experiment 1 may appear rather complex, but its use is simple. It is known as a distillation apparatus. When the vegetable is heated in water in the flask, volatile flavours turn into vapour and pass into the condenser where they are cooled and condense into liquid form. The liquid is collected in the receiver flask when its smell and other properties can be investigated.

Required

Equipment:
3 sets of quick fit distillation apparatus or sets of
    round bottom flasks
    water cooled condenser

Distillation apparatus for investigation of volatile substances

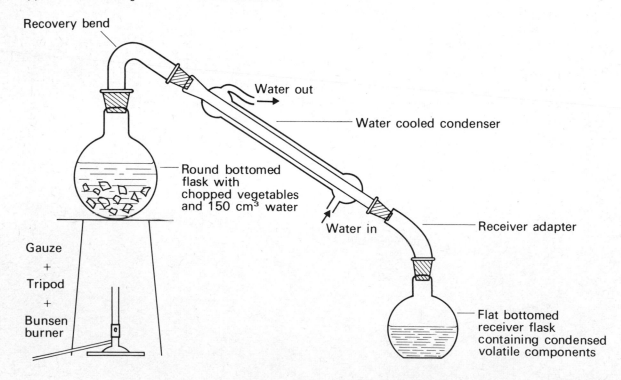

Recovery bend

Water out

Water cooled condenser

Round bottomed flask with chopped vegetables and 150 cm³ water

Gauze
+
Tripod
+
Bunsen burner

Water in

Receiver adapter

Flat bottomed receiver flask containing condensed volatile components

receiver flask and suitable adaptors
tripods, gauzes and bunsen burners
sharp vegetable knives
pans with tight fitting lids or large beakers with clock
    glases
universal indicator pH papers
small beakers
wooden spoon

Materials:
1 kg potatoes
1 kg carrots
1 kg onions
1 kg cabbage
1 kg spinach
1 kg brussels sprouts
4 cooking apples
6 eating apples
sugar
salt

Method

1 Volatile components released on cooking

Assemble 3 sets of distillation equipment starting with a
round bottomed flask of capacity approx. 500 cm^3.
Prepare finely chopped 100 g samples of cabbage, onions
and carrots and transfer these to the round bottom flasks
with 150 cm^3 cold water.
Connect up the apparatus carefully, turn on the water to
the condenser and heat the flask. Allow the contents of
the flask to boil gently for about 30 mins. taking care not
to let it boil dry. Collect any liquid that distils over in a
receiver flask. At the end of the experiment remove the
receiver flasks and smell the contents which are the condensed volatiles.

Which of the three vegetables has the strongest
smell? Is this a desirable or undesirable smell?
Test the pH of the condensed volatiles using pH
paper.
Would the colour of these vegetables be affected
in any way if they were cooked in pans with tight
fitting lids so that the volatiles produced would
remain in the cooking water? (See unit 16).

2 Optimum cooking methods

a *Cooking time.* Prepare approx. 400 g samples of the
following vegetables: potatoes, spinach, Brussels sprouts,
carrots and onions and transfer them to 5 identical pans
each containing 500 cm^3 cold water and 1 level teaspoon
salt. Bring each pan of vegetables to the boil in the same
time and allow to simmer gently without the pan lids on.
Remove a 50 g sample of each vegetable 5 mins. after the
water comes to the boil and transfer it to a small labelled
beaker. Continue removing 50 g samples every 5 mins.
until the vegetables have been simmering 30 mins., taking
care not to let the pans boil dry.
For each vegetable compare the flavour, texture and colour
changes for the different times and decide on the optimum
time to achieve the best results.

b *Quantity of water used and the use of covers on pans.*
Using the results obtained from the previous experiment,
prepare further samples of the vegetable cooked for the
optimum time with the following modifications:
 (i) 500 cm^3 cold water
 (ii) 500 cm^3 boiling water
 (iii) 150 cm^3 cold water
 (iv) 150 cm^3 boiling water
 (v) 500 cm^3 water with a tightly fitting lid on the pan
 (vi) 150 cm^3 water with a tightly fitting lit on the pan
Again compare the flavour, texture and colour variations
for each vegetable.

Does the quantity of water or the presence of
the lid affect the quality of the vegetables in any
way?
From all these observations and with reference to
Unit 16 what recommendations would you make
as to the best method of cooking each of these
vegetables?
Which types of vegetables are best cooked
 (i) in a large amount of water
 (ii) in a small amount of water
 (iii) in a pan without a lid
 (iv) in a pan with a tightly fitting lid?

3 Preparation of apple purée

a Wash, peel and core 2 cooking apples. Cut into slices of
approx. ½ cm width at outer edge and weigh out a 250 g
sample. Transfer to a small pan containing 25 cm^3 water.
Bring to the boil and simmer for approx. 15 mins. until
the slices are soft and tender. Add 50 g sugar and stir with
a wooden spoon to break up the slices until the sugar is
dissolved.

b Repeat **a** using 250 g eating apples cooking for the same
length of time. Three apples may be needed for 250 g.

c Prepare a second sample of 250 g cooking apples and
transfer to a pan containing 50 g sugar already dissolved
in 25 cm^3 water. Bring to the boil, simmer for 15 mins.
and stir with a wooden spoon.

d Repeat **c** using 250 g eating apples.

Compare the colour, texture and flavour of the apple
purées produced.

How do you account for the differences in
texture?

Follow up

Find out the vitamin C content of the vegetables used in
experiment **2**. If the daily recommended intake of vitamin C
per day for all those over the age of 15 is 30 mg calculate the
amount of (a) raw vegetable and (b) cooked vegetable
(assuming 50% vitamin C loss during cooking) that would
need to be eaten to supply a day's intake of the vitamin.
    Which of the vegetables in experiment **2** would you
rate as good sources of vitamin A?

19 Fats and oils

Aims
1 To study some of the properties of a wide variety of fats in order to find which are the most suitable for specific purposes such as frying or spreading.
2 To find the most suitable fat and optimum conditions for preparing creamed cake mixtures.
3 To compare the acceptability of different table fats.

Introduction
Fats and oils are similar to each other in many respects but differ in that whereas fats are solids at normal room temperatures, oils are liquids at such temperatures; in other words fats are distinguished from oils by their melting points. The melting point of a single chemical substance has a fixed value, but fats melt over a range of temperature because they are mixtures. E.g. different types of margarine melt over different temperature ranges depending on the different fats used.

The physical and chemical nature of oils and fats gives them important functions in many different aspects of cooking and food preparation. For example, they are used in frying and for shortening and creaming cakes. They are also used in preparing food emulsions (see unit 27) such as salad cream and icecream.

In the past only a limited range of fats and oils was available - the main fats being butter and lard and the principal oil, olive oil. To-day, by contrast, a whole range of manufactured oils and fats is available made from blends of vegetable, animal and marine fats and oils. It is therefore important to understand how these special purpose products can best be used in cooking.

In making cakes fats are used to help incorporate air into the mixture by *creaming*. When fat and sugar are mixed together or creamed the aim is to incorporate the maximum amount of air into the mixture so that on cooking the mixture will be properly aerated, producing a light and tender product. As more air is incorporated into a creamed fat its density falls, and this suggests one way of measuring the effect of creaming (experiment 2). Fats designed to have good creaming powers are now available and usually incorporate *monoglycerides* such as glyceryl monostearate (see unit 27) to improve their emulsifying power.

Fats and oils are used for frying because they enable high temperatures to be used and because they can be heated almost to their boiling point without much decomposition occurring. During frying, fats and oils should not be heated above their *smoke point,* which is the temperature they start to break down, producing an acrid odour and imparting an unpleasant flavour to the food. It is desirable that a fat used for frying should have a high smoke point so that it can be used at high temperatures. Various factors lower the smoke point including the following:
(a) the presence of emulsifiers in the fat
(b) the presence of particles of food in the fat
(c) repeated use of the fat
(d) large surface area of fat.

Note. Take care when heating fats and do not heat above the smoke point.

Required

Equipment:
narrow capillary tubes
thermometers — 0-110°C (in 0.2°C divisions)
thermometers — 0-360°C
small rubber bands or $^1/_5$ cm rings cut from rubber tubing
1000 cm³ beakers
clamp and stands
bunsen burners and tripods
small bowls or basins
wooden spoons
wide necked density bottles or small glass jars
knife
stopclock
graph paper
rotary hand whisk
electric mixer
use of refrigerator
small frying pans or evaporating basins
accurate electrical balance

Materials:
a wide variety of animal and vegetable fats and oils
   including: lard, suet, butter, different margarines, low
   calorie spread etc.
granulated sugar
caster sugar
icing sugar
sliced bread

Method
1 **Melting points of different fats**
   Use as wide a variety of animal and vegetable fats as possible in this experiment.
   e.g. animal fats: beef suet, mutton fat, lard,
                      2 brands of butter e.g. Danish, New
                      Zealand
        vegetable fats: hydrogenated vegetable cooking fats
                         hard baking margarine
                         soft luxury margarine,
                         poly-unsaturated margarine
                         low calorie slimming spread
   Melt a small portion of each fat and draw up into a capillary tube. Seal one end of the tube with a bunsen flame and then allow the fat to cool for several hours in a refrigerator. Prepare at least 2 tubes of each fat to be tested and make sure that you know which tubes contain which fat. Attach each tube to the bulb of a thermometer using a small rubber band or ring and suspend the thermometer so that the bulb is in the centre of a 1 litre beaker full of water. The thermometer should not touch the sides or bottom

of the beaker.

Adjust the bunsen burner to produce a low flame and very gradually heat up the water watching the fat sample all the time. The fat may soften and move in the tube, but the melting point is the temperature reached when the fat becomes clear. Record this temperature and repeat with the duplicate fat sample. If the melting points of the 2 samples are not the same, repeat with a third sample until a consistent result is achieved. Compare the melting points of the different fats with each other and with published values if available.

Why do some of the fats melt over a temperature range rather than at one distinct temperature?

What accounts for this difference in melting points of the fats and how is this related to their consistency at room temperature?

Do these differing melting points put any restrictions on to the use of certain fats?

2 Creaming of fats

Again use a wide range of animal and vegetable fats for this experiment.

e.g. animal fats: lard, butter

vegetable fats: hydrogenated cooking fat
different margarines — hard, soft, whipped
low calorie slimming spread

a *Optimum creaming times for different fats.*

Calculate the volume of a wide necked density bottle or small glass cylinder by weighing it empty, weighing it full of water and subtracting the 2 figures to obtain the weight of water.

Assuming 1 g of water occupies 1 cm^3, the volume of the container can be worked out.

Stir 50 g sugar into 50 g of one of the fats and immediately remove sufficient of the mixture to fill the container and then weigh it.

Density of mixture =

$$\frac{\text{Wt. of mixture} - \text{Wt. of container}}{\text{volume of container}}$$

Return the sample to the initial mixture and clean the container. Cream the fat/sugar mixture with a wooden spoon for exactly 5 minutes before removing a sample to measure its density as above. Return the sample to the mixture and repeat the procedure for 3 further periods of 5 minutes to give a total creaming time of 20 minutes. Plot a simple graph of density against creaming time. Repeat this using a wide range of fats as suggested at the beginning, and plot similar graphs.

By comparing the fall in density over the time range, decide on an optimum creaming time for each fat, and also choose the fat which would give the best results — i.e. produces the lowest density in the shortest time.

What are the disadvantages of using (a) lard and (b) a low calorie spread in creaming mixtures? Can you think of reasons why they behave in this way?

Do the whipped margarines have any advantages over the ordinary soft margarines?

b *Creaming methods.* Repeat experiment a using just two of the fats e.g. a hard and soft margarine but use different methods of creaming:

 (i) with a wooden spoon

 (ii) with a rotary hand whisk

(iii) with an electric mixer.

Compare the density results for the different methods in order to decide whether these pieces of equipment could be used to give better results or to reduce the creaming time necessary.

c *Temperature of the fat.* Repeat experiment a again using two of the fats e.g. hard and soft margarine but start with them at different temperatures:

 (i) straight from the refrigerator (approximately 5°C)

 (ii) room temperature (approximately 15°C)

(iii) slightly warmer (approximately 25° to 30°C)

(iv) melted

With reference to the density results, decide on the optimum temperature for creaming of a fat.

d *Different sugars.* Repeat experiment a using two of the fats e.g. hard and soft margarine but use different types of sugar:

 (i) icing sugar

 (ii) caster sugar

(iii) granulated sugar

Again decide on the best type of sugar for efficient creaming.

The use of different amounts of fat in a cake showing the effect of too little (right), too much (centre) compared with the control (left). (See unit 15)

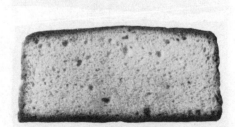

3 Frying temperatures

a *Type of fat.* Take 50 g samples of a variety of different fats and oils e.g. lard, hydrogenated vegetable fat, butter, margarine, low calorie spread and at least 3 different cooking oils. Put the fat into a small frying pan or porcelain evaporating basin and gently heat noticing any changes which take place and the temperature at which they occur. *Use extreme care to prevent the fat setting on fire, and stop the experiment when the fat starts spitting a lot or giving off a thin bluish smoke.*
Bearing in mind that fairly high temperatures are required for efficient frying of foods, decide which of the fats tested would be most suitable for frying.

What are the disadvantages of using butter or margarine for frying?
Why does it state 'Do not use for frying'' on the labels of low calorie spreads?
What would be the effect of frying chips in a fat which breaks down at a low temperature?

b *Effect of constant reuse of frying oils.* Heat approximately 50 g of cooking oil in a small frying pan until a faint smoke can be seen to rise from it *(take care).* Stop heating and record the temperature, using a 360°C thermometer. Drop a small square (1 cm) of bread into the fat, record the time it takes to fry, remove and examine when cool.
Allow the oil to cool, and then repeat the above experiment five times heating until faint smoke appears, frying the bread and cooling.
Record the different smoke temperatures, time of frying and also the colour of the oil and fried bread.

Repeat the experiment using different cooking oils and compare the results.

What is the effect of constantly reheating certain oils to their smoking point?
What recommendations would you make as to the best way of using a frying oil in order to minimise these changes and hence increase its useful life?

4 Table fats

Spread a slice of white bread evenly with one of the table fats and divide up into small squares and put on a clean plate. Repeat this for a range of fats such as salted and unsalted butter, hard margarine, polyunsaturated margarine and low calorie spread. Label the different samples in a random way and invite others to taste them.
The tasters may be asked to identify the fats, pick out those which are butter or alternatively rank them in order of preference. A triangle test (see unit 24) may be used to detect small differences between samples or to check how many people can actually differentiate butter from margarine.

What are the essential characteristics of an ideal table fat?
Find out the prices of the different fats used and based on this and the results of the tasting experiment, decide on a best buy.
What are the possible health advantages of margarine which claim to be high in polyunsaturated fatty acids?

Creaming may be done by hand (left), using a rotary hand whisk (centre), or an electric mixer (right); (see 2b).

 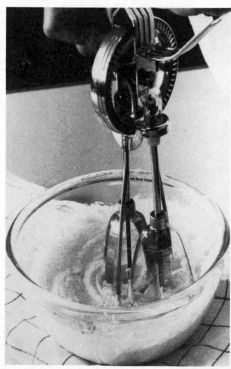 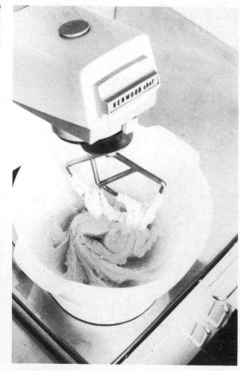

Follow up
Using the information on a packet of low calorie slimming
spread compare the energy value of the spread with that of
butter and margarine. From the energy value work out the
approximate fat content of the low calorie spread. What else
do you think the spread contains? Note the other ingredients
in the spread and work out why they are there.
What are the disadvantages of low calorie spreads when used
(a) for frying and (b) creaming?

20 Sugar and sugar confectionery

Aims

1 To investigate the properties of sugar solutions when heated.
2 To look at the factors which affect the crystallisation of sugar and to apply these to the production of various types of sugar confectionery.

Introduction

Sugar or sucrose is the main ingredient in all sugar confectionery which is made by boiling a concentrated sugar solution i.e. a syrup. When a syrup boils, water evaporates thus increasing the concentration of the solution and raising the boiling point. Hard confectionery such as butterscotch and boiled sweets contain very little water and are produced by boiling to a high temperature, whereas soft confectionery such as caramel contain more water and is boiled to a lower temperature.

All sugar confectionery is produced by controlled crystallisation of sucrose from a very strong sugar solution, but a distinction is made between *non-crystalline* and *crystalline* sugar confectionery according to the extent to which crystallisation of sucrose has occurred.

Strong sucrose solutions normally crystallise on cooling but this can be prevented if a small amount of an acid such as tartaric acid is added. The acid causes some *inversion* of the sucrose to occur i.e.

sucrose + acid $\longrightarrow$ glucose + fructose.

Glucose does not crystallise easily and it inhibits the crystallisation of sucrose. *Fehling's test* can be used to find out whether inversion has occurred because the test is positive with glucose and fructose but negative with sucrose.

Toffee differs from boiled sweets in that it contains a high proportion of ingredients other than sugar such as milk and fat. It consists of tiny droplets of fat dispersed in a very strong sugar solution. The colour and flavour of toffee comes mainly from the *caramelization* of the milk solids that occurs during cooking and the interaction of milk proteins with sugar. Some inversion of sucrose is necessary to prevent crystallisation. The hardness of toffee depends on the temperature to which it is boiled.

Fondant, which is the creamy material used as soft centres in chocolates, is an example of crystalline confectionery. In essence it consists of minute sugar crystals dispersed in a very strong sugar solution. Crystallisation has to be carefully controlled by rapid cooling and vigorous mixing to prevent the formation of large crystals which produce a dry, crumbly texture. The presence of a *small* amount of invert sugar helps to keep the crystals small.

Required

Equipment:
small enamel pans or evaporating basins
1000 cm^3 beakers
100 cm^3 measuring cylinders
foil trays
asbestos mats
wooden spoons, tablespoons
thermometers to measure up to 200°C or special sugar boiling thermometers
microscopes plus slides and coverslips
test tubes, scales or balance
earthenware basins
bunsen burners and tripods or gas/electric rings

Materials:
sugar, granulated or caster
glucose
cream of tartar
tartaric acid
sodium bicarbonate
dilute hydrochloric acid
dilute sodium hydroxide
Fehlings solutions I and II
brown sugar
butter
golden syrup
condensed skimmed milk

Method

1 The effect of temperature on a sugar solution

a *Colour.* Mix a small amount of sugar — approximately 30 g — with 15 cm^3 of water in an evaporating dish. Heat gently until the solution boils, stirring only until all the sugar has completely dissolved. Note the temperature at which the solution boils and then continue heating noticing any changes in the colour and smell of the solution and recording the temperatures at which these changes occur. Continue heating until the sugar forms charcoal.

b *Texture and flavour.* Repeat a using 100 g sugar with 50 cm^3 water gently heated to boiling. Continue heating and using an accurate (e.g. sugar boiling) thermometer pour out a small sample of the solution at 10°C intervals (e.g. 110°C, 120°C, 130°C etc. up to 180°C) into cold water to cool it. Remove the samples from the water and squeeze between the fingers to see whether the lump of sugar forms into threads, a soft ball or is very brittle. Taste the samples and comment on the flavour and texture.

How does increasing the temperature affect the colour, flavour and texture of these sugar samples?
From your results decide on suitable boiling temperatures for producing (i) fondant (ii) barley sugar and (iii) toffee.
Is the flavour of the very dark brown caramel acceptable?
Where could this product be of use in the kitchen?

2 The role of invert sugar in crystallisation

a *Fehlings Test.* Dissolve a small amount of sugar in water in a test tube according to the modifications below. Add equal volumes of Fehlings solutions I and II, shake well and warm gently noticing any change in colour.

(i) ordinary granulated sugar (sucrose)

(ii) sugar boiled with a few drops of dilute hydrochloric acid and neutralised with caustic soda solution before testing

(iii) sugar boiled with a pinch of tartaric acid or cream of tartar and neutralised as in (ii)

(iv) glucose

What is the effect of heating sugar with acid?

b *Crystallisation.* Warm 40 g granulated sugar with 15 cm^3 water until a clear solution is obtained. Divide into two separate evaporating dishes and add a pinch of tartaric acid to one before continuing heating both for a few minutes. Allow to cool and observe which sample crystallises out.

How does the acid affect crystallisation and to what types of confectionery should you add it?

3 The production of non-crystalline confectionery

a *Barley sugar.* Dissolve 100 g granulated sugar in 50 cm^3 water and heat in a smooth sided saucepan, e.g. enamel, stirring until all the sugar has dissolved. At approximately 115°C add 0.2 g tartaric acid and continue heating until the solution turns a pale straw colour. Pour a small portion of the solution onto a greased foil sheet to cool and continue heating the rest until it turns a golden colour. Immediately pour this onto a second foil dish and allow to cool. Compare the nature of the two samples and decide which you prefer.

While the mixture is still soft but not too hot, thin strips may be pulled into fine strands of barley sugar or twisted into sticks.

What would have been the effect of heating the solution until it was a very dark golden colour before cooling?

Explain the role of tartaric acid in the recipe and the effects of omitting it.

b *Honeycombe crunch.* Repeat **a** but add a mixture of 3 g tartaric acid and 3 g sodium bicarbonate to the sugar solution when pale golden. Stir rapidly before pouring into the greased dishes to cool and observe the changes in texture.

What has caused the development of the honeycomb texture?

c *Toffee.* Blend together the following until smooth:
70 g condensed milk
30 g sugar
20 g golden syrup

Dissolve 50 g sugar (preferably brown) in 20 cm^3 water and heat to a temperature of 115°C, using a sugar boiling thermometer. Add this to the milk mixture and stir well. Immediately remove two level tablespoonfuls of the mixture and put in a small greased foil dish to cool.
Cook the remaining mixture very gently stirring all the time until the temperature is 120°C, and then remove 2 tablespoonfuls of the mixture as before. Continue heating the mixture removing further samples at 130°C, 140°C and 150°C. Allow all the samples to cool completely before examining them. Compare the colour, flavour, chewiness and brittleness of all samples before deciding on the optimum temperature for cooking toffee.

What is the effect of using (a) a lower and (b) a higher temperature when making toffee?
Why is citric acid sometimes added to a toffee mixture?

4 The production of crystalline confectionery e.g. fondant
Basic recipe: 100 g granulated sugar
50 cm^3 water
0.1 g cream of tartar

Heat these in a small smooth sided pan stirring only to ensure complete dissolving, until the temperature reaches exactly 115°C. Carefully pour the mixture into a smooth earthenware basin and allow to cool to 40°C. Beat the mixture vigorously with a wooden spoon until it becomes thick and creamy. When it is too stiff to beat, knead the mixture into a smooth, velvety mass. Transfer a tiny sample of the completed fondant to a microscope slide with a coverslip and examine the crystal size under a magnification of approximately 200.

Modifications

a *Effect of beating temperature.* Prepare 2 samples of fondant as above but allow one sample to cool to 70°C before beating, and beat the other immediately.

b *Effect of cream of tartar.* Prepare 2 samples of fondant as above but omit the cream of tartar from one and add 0.4 g to the other.
Compare the textures, including mouth feel, of all the samples and also their relative crystal size.

What is the advantage of cooling the mixture to 40°C prior to beating?
Why is a substance inhibiting crystallisation e.g. cream of tartar added to a crystalline sweet such as fondant?
Why is the amount used critical?
Why is it important to use smooth sided vessels throughout and to avoid any dust or dirt getting in the mixture?

Follow up

1 Consider the sweet 'fudge' and decide whether it is crystalline or non crystalline and how you think it might be manufactured. Try and design a simple method of producing fudge in the laboratory/kitchen.

21 Novel protein products I
– rehydration of dry products

Aims
1 To compare the different methods of rehydrating various kinds of dry vegetable protein foods.
2 To measure the increase in weight during rehydration.
3 To compare the flavour of the products rehydrated in different solutions.

Introduction
The world shortage and cost of animal protein has led to a search for sources of cheaper vegetable protein that could replace animal protein in the diet. Unfortunately the quality of most vegetable protein is much lower than that of animal protein, though there is one notable exception, namely soya beans. Soya bean products provide an acceptable alternative to meat because the amino acid content of soya bean protein compares well with that of beef protein, apart from its lower content of methionine and to a lesser extent lysine. (The biological value of soya protein is 70 compared to a value of 75 for meat).

In addition supplies of soya beans are readily available as they are grown extensively and cheaply in many areas of the world, but particularly in the U.S.A.

Soya bean flour may be converted into products that have many similarities to meat. One of the best known of these is texturised vegetable protein, TVP. This is made by passing a mixture of defatted soya flour, additives and water through an extruder at a high temperature and pressure. The result is a dried product containing about 8% moisture that has a chewy texture. TVP is available in many shapes and sizes,

Soya beans are a useful source of good quality protein.

including chunks, flakes and granules, in both unflavoured and flavoured forms. Another product made by spinning protein extracted from soya beans has a more meat-like texture than the texturised product but has the disadvantage that it is more expensive.

Most soya bean products are produced in dried form and the acceptability of the hydrated food depends very much on how the hydration is carried out. In the experiments that follow the effect of the type of product and size of piece, the time of hydration, the temperature of the water, and the effect of adding different flavouring substances to the water are investigated.

It should be noted that when comparing the nutritional value or cost of soya products with meat (or other protein food) the hydrated and not the dried product should be used. Although the keeping qualities of dried soya foods are excellent, once they are hydrated they are perishable foods with keeping qualities similar to those of fresh meat.

Required

Equipment:
large beakers or small pans
tripods, gauzes and bunsen burners
or gas/electric rings
scales or electric balance

Materials:
textured vegetable protein products of different sizes
    e.g. TVP* – mince, granules and chunks
spun vegetable protein products of different sizes
    e.g. Kesp* – mince and chunks
stock cubes
Marmite or Bovril
curry powder or paste
salt, pepper
fruit juice e.g. orange
tomato juice or puree

*See Appendix 1 for details of manufacturers.

Method
1 Rehydration times and techniques

a Weigh out 20 g samples of each product available and record accurately the weight of each. Transfer each sample to a large beaker or small pan and add 200 cm³ of cold water. Stir well and leave to stand for 10 minutes. Drain off the excess water and reweigh each sample, recording the new weight. Return the partially rehydrated product to the beaker or pan and add 200 cm³ of water. Leave to stand for a further 10 mins., drain off excess water and again reweigh the sample. Repeat this process a third time so that the sample has been in contact with the water for a total of 30 mins. If there is a significant difference between the last two weights for any sample, repeat this for a further 10 mins. in order to obtain a constant weight.

Soya bean flour that has been spun into fibres to give it a meat-like texture.

(**Note** Some of the larger sized pieces require a long hydration time).
Express the new weight of the samples at each stage as a fraction of the original weight, e.g. if sample now weighs 60 g, this is 3 times the original weight.

b Repeat **a** for each sample, this time adding boiling water at each stage in place of cold water and allow to stand.

c Repeat **a** for each sample, this time adding boiling water at each stage and simmering for each 10 minute period.

d Repeat **a** for each sample adding 200 cm³ cold water and leaving to soak overnight if possible.

Tabulate all your results and compare the relative effectiveness of each method of rehydration.

Which method do you consider to be the best for each type of product used?
For each product used, find out from the manufacturer their recommended method of rehydration and see if this agrees with your conclusions.
Which sample absorbed the most water?
How does this affect the nutritional value of the hydrated product?

Again with reference to the nutritional information supplied by the manufacturer for both dry and hydrated products, work out whether their figures for the hydrated products are the same as yours.

2 Rehydration in different solutions
For these experiments choose approx. four different samples e.g.

a spun protein beef mince

b textured protein brown beef chunks

c textured protein brown unflavoured mince

d textured protein neutral unflavoured granules

For each sample choose the most effective rehydration method from **1** amd rehydrate approx. 20 g of the dry product in 200 cm³ water with the following additions:
 (i) control, no addition
 (ii) ½ stock cube
 (iii) 1 tsp. Marmite or Bovril
 (iv) 1 tsp. curry powder or paste
 (v) good pinch of salt and pepper
 (vi) 2 tsp. tomato puree, or 200 cm³ tomato juice
 (vii) replace water with 200 cm³ fruit juice for neutral granules only.
Compare each flavoured sample with the control sample and decide whether you think it is an improvement or not. Suggest suitable meals where these products could be used and state how you would rehydrate the dry samples in each case.

Can you think of any foods where you could use the neutral unflavoured granules in their dry state?

Follow up
1 Compare the ease and speed of hydration of TVP with that of other dried convenience foods, such as potatoes, coffee, soups and puddings.
2 Find out the extent to which TVP is being used in schools, colleges and hospitals in your area. Try to find out also the ways in which it is being used.

22 Novel protein products II –experimental cookery

Aims
1 To compare the use of textured and spun proteins as an alternative to meat.
2 To find the most acceptable level for using textured vegetable protein in meat dishes.
3 To introduce the hedonic scale as a method of assessing food products.

Introduction
Soya protein foods are finding increasing uses. TVP is now regularly used in schools, canteens and hospitals while the more expensive spun product is mainly used in hotels, restaurants and industrial canteens. Whereas a spun protein such as Kesp is intended to be used on its own in place of meat, TVP is normally used as a 'meat extender' by replacing a proportion of the meat in traditional meat dishes. TVP is also being used in simulated meat products, such as curry, burger and banger-style mixes that are often sold in Health Food stores and which are particularly suitable for vegetarians. There is no doubt that the use of vegetable protein foods will increase in the future, partly because of their low cost compared with most meat, and partly because improved products and recipes will be developed.

In this unit several dishes are to be cooked — and recipes may be modified according to personal preference — and the results are to be assessed subjectively. One simple way of expressing personal preference is to use the *hedonic scale* — that is a scale that expresses the extent of the taster's like or dislike for the food. The hedonic scale expresses degree of like or dislike on a 9-point scale as follows:

Points	Extent of like or dislike
9	like extremely
8	like very much
7	like moderately
6	like slightly
5	neither like nor dislike
4	dislike slightly
3	dislike moderately
2	dislike very much
1	dislike extremely

If a number of people taste a particular dish the use of the hedonic scale gives a simple means of establishing the nature of personal preference.

Required

Equipment:
pans
electric/gas rings plus ovens
sharp vegetable knives
wooden spoons
knives, forks, spoons
measuring jugs
scales
small pie dishes e.g. 10 cm x 20 cm x 4 cm foil dishes
chopping boards
vegetable peelers
rolling pins
basins

Materials:
spun vegetable protein e.g. Kesp*
textured vegetable protein e.g. TVP*
onions
tomato puree
apples
stock cubes
carrots
peas
curry powder
sultanas
chutney
potatoes
gravy browing
cooking oil
mixed vegetables
flaky pastry
salt, pepper
stewing steak
minced beef
spaghetti
sausage meat
mixed herbs
long grain rice
grated cheese

* See Appendix 1 for details of manufacturers.

Method
1 Use of textured and spun protein as an alternative to meat

a *Curry.* Prepare a mild sweet curry using approximately 100 g onions, 25 g apple, 25 g chutney, 25 g sultanas, 2 tsp. curry powder, 1 stock cube, tomato purée, salt, pepper and flour for thickening as required, and cooking oil.
 (i) use 40 g dry textured beef flavoured chunks rehydrated prior to use in 200 cm^3 water containing 1 tsp. curry powder.
 (ii) use 75 g dry spun beef flavoured chunks rehydrated prior to use in 200 cm^3 water containing 1 tsp. curry powder. Serve with boiled rice.

b *Spaghetti bolognese.* Prepare a bolognese sauce using approximately 100 g onions, 50 g mushrooms, 25 g carrots, 50 g tomato purée, 1 stock cube, herbs, salt, pepper and flour for thickening as required, and cooking oil.
 (i) use 40 g dry textured beef flavoured mince rehydrated prior to use in 200 cm^3 water containing 1 tsp. tomato purée.

(ii) use 75 g dry spun beef flavoured mince rehydrated prior to use in 200 cm^3 water containing 1 tsp. tomato purée. Serve with spaghetti and grated cheese.

Assess these dishes using the hedonic scale (see Introduction) Get others in the class to taste the dishes and record their results. Compare their results with your own.

Do you find these recipes acceptable? How would you describe the texture of the protein pieces?

2   Use of textured vegetable protein to replace a certain amount of meat

a *Savoury mince dishes.* Prepare a savoury mince type stew using approximately 100 g onions, gravy browning, ½ stock cube, cooking oil, salt and pepper to taste and flour for thickening if required.
  (i) use 150 g minced beef
 (ii) use 100 g minced beef plus 15 g dry textured vegetable 'mince' protein rehydrated in approximately 100 cm^3 water containing stock, seasoning or Marmite as desired
(iii) use 50 g minced beef plus 30 g dry vegetable textured 'mince' rehydrated as above
(iv) use 50 g dry textured vegetable 'mince' rehydrated as above.
  This type of recipe may be modified to produce various dishes e.g.
    shepherds pie — with mashed potato topping
    meat pie — with mixed vegetable and flaky pastry topping
    cornish pasty — with mixed vegetable and diced potato in pastry case — the chunky products could be used here with stewing steak.

Whichever modification is used, prepare all 4 alternatives using the different ratios of meat: vegetable protein in exactly the same way and assess on the hedonic scale as in experiment **1.**

b *Sausage based products.* Using fresh pork sausage meat, mix it well with rehydrated neutral unflavoured textured protein granules in the proportions suggested below adding extra seasoning as the percentage of the latter increases. Mould this mix into round flat sausage cakes, coat with flour and fry or roll into floured sausage shapes, coat in pastry to make sausage rolls and cook in a hot oven.
  (i) use 200 g fresh sausage
 (ii) use 150 g fresh sausage plus 15 g dry neutral unflavoured textured granules rehydrated in seasoned water
(iii) use 100 g fresh sausage plus 30 g dry granules rehydrated as above
(iv) use 50 g fresh sausage plus 45 g dry granules rehydrated as above.
  Again assess on the hedonic scale. Notice any difference in the appearance of the four batches of sausage rolls.

Can you detect the presence of the textured protein in these dishes? If so, was it because of the texture, colour or flavour?
Suggest modifications to the recipe to improve your product.
What do you think is the most acceptable level of replacement when using textured protein products?
Find out what are the manufacturer's recommendations for using these products and compare these with your own.

Follow up
1 Find out the price of fresh minced beef and pork sausage meat from the butchers and also the price of the textured vegetable protein products you have used. Assuming that the recipes above in **2** provide 4 children's portions; work out the cost of using all meat for 100 portions. Repeat your calculations using the proportions of meat and TVP you found acceptable.
  How much money would you save?
  Find out how many lunches your school or college conteen prepares each day and calculate how much money would be saved if the cook used your recommended amount of textured protein once a week.
2 The dry neutral unflavoured granules are a very versatile product. Try out the following ideas and then think of some different ones.

a Rehydrate in fruit juice, mix with apple purée and use to make apple crumble.

b Use dry as a crumble topping or a crunchy flan case.

c Add dry to muesli type breakfast cereals.

d Rehydrate in water with salt and pepper and mixed herbs. Mix with grated cheese and use as an alternative to sausage meat in sausage rolls or scotch eggs.

An appetising casserole made from spun vegetable protein in the form of beef-flavoured chunks.

23 Convenience foods I–vitamin C content

Aims

1 To investigate the effect of preservation on the Vitamin C content of vegetables.
2 To discover whether the various types of fruit drinks available are a significant source of Vitamin C.

Introduction

In unit 17 we noted the importance of fruit and vegetables as a source of Vitamin C, and as fruit and vegetables are being bought increasingly in convenience (i.e. preserved) form it is important to know how the process of preservation affects the Vitamin C content.

It is evident from unit 17 that Vitamin C is easily destroyed. It is destroyed by oxygen in the air, by moderate temperatures, and it is also lost by solution into water. For these reasons Vitamin C is vulnerable to any method of preservation (and cooking).

The main methods of preserving fruit and vegetables are drying, freezing, freeze drying or canning and all these methods involve some loss of Vitamin C. Whichever method is used the fruit or vegetable is usually blanched i.e. treated with hot water for up to 5 minutes before being preserved. Blanching destroys enzymes and softens texture but is also the main cause of loss of Vitamin C (typically between 20% and 30%). Freezing and freeze drying cause little further loss of Vitamin C, though with canning further loss is unavoidable due to the relatively long time for which cans are heated. In addition, canned food loses more Vitamin C on storage because of the presence of oxygen in the 'headspace' of the can. Food dried in air also loses Vitamin C, though modern quick-drying and vacuum-drying methods have reduced this loss.

The Vitamin C content of peas, whether canned, frozen (centre) or dried (experiment 1a), is reduced during preservation mainly due to blanching.

In general, frozen and freeze dried fruit and vegetables should contain at least as much Vitamin C as fresh ones — and possibly more if the so-called fresh variety was harvested several days before purchase. Canned and dried fruits and vegetables may contain rather less Vitamin C than fresh ones, but the difference is not usually great.

Required

Equipment:
100 cm³ measuring cylinder
50 cm³ burettes
5 cm³ pipettes
10 cm³ pipettes
20 cm³ pipettes
100 cm³ graduated flasks
100 cm³ conical flasks
250 cm³ measuring cylinders
muslin cloths
lemon squeezer
sharp vegetable knives
liquidizer
small pans or large beakers
gas/electric rings or bunsen burners
can opener
basin
electric balance or scales

Materials:
100 cm³ ascorbic acid solution made up as in unit 17 experiment **1b** (0.2mg/cm³)
2000 cm³ 2:6 dichlorophenol indophenol solution made up as in unit 17 experiment **1a** (0.2mg/cm³) and standardized as in experiment **1c**.
2000 cm³ metaphosphoric acid 20% solution
acetone
fresh peas
quick frozen peas
canned garden peas
canned processed peas
AFD instant peas
quick dried peas
marrow fat dried peas
fresh sprouts
quick frozen sprouts
canned sprouts (if available)
fresh potatoes
canned potatoes
dried potato enriched with Vitamin C
ordinary dried potato
fresh orange
frozen orange juice
canned orange juice
orange squash 'with extra Vitamin C'
ordinary orange squash
dried orange juice

Method

1 Vitamin C content of preserved vegetables

a *Peas.* Use the method described in Unit 17 experiment **3** to determine the Vitamin C content of the different types of peas available. Compare the Vitamin C content of fresh, frozen, and canned peas before cooking, using 50 g samples. Rehydrate the dried peas as directed on the packet and cook all the samples for their recommended lengths of time before measuring the Vitamin C content of these different ready to eat peas.

How do you account for the difference between the fresh and frozen peas?
Which method of preservation has
  (i) retained
 (ii) destroyed
the most Vitamin C? Can you give reasons for this?

Calculate the amount of Vitamin C in an average serving — approx. 75 g — of cooked peas and decide which of these products can be said to be a significant source of the vitamin.

b *Sprouts.* Repeat experiment **a** using fresh, frozen and canned sprouts before and after cooking.
Give reasons for the results obtained.

c *Potatoes.* Measure the Vitamin C content of cooked potatoes as in experiment **a** using fresh, canned, dried (enriched with Vitamin C) and ordinary dried potatoes.

Fresh; peel, cut into pieces and boil for 15-20 mins. until soft. Mash half the sample and retain the other half.
Dried; rehydrate both dried samples as directed on the packets.
Canned; heat the canned potatoes as directed on the can.

Measure the Vitamin C content of the 5 samples namely: boiled, mashed, 2 rehydrated and canned, and compare the results.

Has the process of mashing the fresh potato affected the Vitamin C content? Can you think of any reasons for this?
Has the addition of extra Vitamin C to the dried potato mix during manufacture had any effect on the Vitamin C content of the final product?

Calculate the Vitamin C content of a 100 g portion of each cooked potato and decide whether any of these are a significant source of the vitamin.

Follow up

Work out the cost of a portion of each of the peas used in experiment **1 a**, making allowances for the increase in weight on rehydration for the dried peas.
  Taking into account their nutritional value, ease of preparation and availability or storage requirements, which of these 'convenience food' type products is the best value for money? From the flavour and texture of these different peas, which would you buy?

Repeat the above exercise for the sprouts and potatoes in order to assess their convenience value.

2 Comparison of fruit drinks

Use the method described in unit 17 experiment **2** to compare the Vitamin C content of different orange drinks. Use 20 cm^3 samples of the fresh, canned and frozen juices. Rehydrate the dried mix as described on the packet before use. Use the undiluted orange squash first and then after dilution to the correct strength.

Note. 2 cm^3 acetone should be added to the conical flask after addition of 10 cm^3 juice before titration of all the preserved juices to counteract the effect of the sulphur dioxide used as preservative.

Calculate the Vitamin C content of a 100 cm^3 portion of each drink — diluted as recommended for the undiluted samples. Give reasons for any differences.

Can these undiluted fruit squashes claim to be a significant source of Vitamin C in the diet?
Does the inclusion of 'extra Vitamin C' make much difference?

Follow up

Find out the prices of the different fruit drinks used. Bearing in mind your experimental results — comment on their value. Try and find out the difference between a fruit squash, a fruit drink and a fruit-flavoured drink.

24 Convenience foods II – value for money

Aims

1 To assess the value of convenience mixes as compared to home made products.
2 To investigate the various instant desserts available.

Introduction

A convenience food is one made in a factory so that the skills of preparation are applied in the factory rather than the home. This relieves the housewife of the work and time formerly involved in preparing food in the home. Although convenience foods may involve little or no time, effort and skill in preparation such foods are usually more expensive than home-made ones. Semi-prepared foods such as cake mixes and dried instant desserts differ from complete convenience foods in that some preparation is still left to the housewife.

In the experiments that follow home-made products are compared with corresponding convenience foods in a number of ways so that the merits of each can be assessed. Such an assessment must by its nature be subjective and it is important that the investigator approaches this with an open mind and tries not to indulge in personal prejudice. For example, if a person who is comparing a home-made product with a convenience one is biased in favour of one or the other before assessing them, the results are not likely to be valid!

One method of subjective assessment is to express the extent of like or dislike of a food using the *Hedonic scale* described in unit 22. In experiment **2** of this unit such a method may be used to rank different instant puddings in order of preference.

Another way of assessing foods — and a very simple way — is to establish whether any *difference* exists between samples. One way of doing this is by means of the *triangle test.* In this test 3 samples are used, two being identical, and the taster is asked to identify the different one. This test is especially useful when the differences between samples is likely to be small, as in the case of different makes of instant desserts. Such a test reveals differences between samples, but does not give any indication of the nature of the differences. If this is required further questions must be asked. As only 2 different samples are used in the triangle test there is a chance (one in three) of guessing the answer correctly. Therefore unless the majority of the tasters — at least half — give the correct answer, the result is not significant.

Required

Equipment:
mixing bowls
wooden spoons
tablespoons
cake tins, teaspoons
greaseproof paper
knives
rotary or hand whisk
100 cm³ measuring cylinder
stop clock
large measuring cylinder e.g. 2000 cm³
large rectangular box
shallow tray
small custard cups or dishes
gas/electric rings or bunsen burners
oven

Materials:
margarine
sugar, salt
self raising flour
eggs
milk
cocoa powder
chocolate cake mix — at least 3 different types
1 bought chocolate cake
Bird's Angel Delight — raspberry flavoured
at least 3 'own brand' raspberry flavoured desserts
creme caramel mixes — several types
rice

Method

1 Comparison of convenience foods with the home-made equivalent

a *Chocolate cakes.* In this experiment an ordinary chocolate sandwich cake is compared with various convenience cake mixes. If possible obtain mixes where;

 (i) only water is added
 (ii) water plus an egg is added
 (iii) several ingredients are added e.g. sugar, egg, fat.
    Prepare a basic chocolate sandwich cake according to the following recipe and the method in Unit 15 experiment **1**:
    50 g margarine
    50 g caster sugar
    38 g self raising flour
    12 g cocoa powder
    1 egg.
    Carefully record the total preparation time and then bake in a well greased tin for approx. 30 mins. at 180°C. For each of the packet cake mixes, follow the instructions on the packet carefully and again record the preparation time and bake as directed. When the cakes are cool compare them with the bought cake (if possible a simple un-iced cake) on the following basis:
  (i) Price: remember to include the other ingredients for the cake mixes. Work out the price for the whole cake and also for a 50 g portion.
 (ii) Weight:
 (iii) Volume: this may be determined visually or by measurement, using the seed displacement method as follows:
    Fill a large rectangular box standing in a shallow tray full to overflowing with dried rice. Level the top carefully with a ruler and then estimate the volume of the box by measuring the volume of the seeds contained in it using the large

measuring cylinder (Volume V1).

Put one of the cakes in the box, refill with rice and level the top. Measure the volume of the rice again (volume V2) and hence calculate the volume of the cake (V1-V2).

(iv) Overall size and shape (visual check)
(v) Colour, external and internal
(vi) Texture (open, close, uneven etc.)
(vii) Taste
(viii) Preparation time and cooking time
(ix) Storage requirements.

Notice any particular advantage of each cake and then on the basis of the above results work out which cake is the best value for money.

Do you consider it is worthwhile the housewife baking her own chocolate cakes when these mixes and also ready made chocolate cakes are available?

b *Crème caramel.* Another product which sometimes takes a long time to prepare is crème caramel and today there are a number of 'convenience' methods of producing this sweet.

If possible obtain the following types:
(i) ready made frozen product
(ii) ready made refrigerated product
(iii) well known dried mix complete with caramel topping
(iv) 'own brand' dried mix with caramel topping.

Prepare the basic product using the egg custard recipe from Unit 9 experiment 1 using the following:

200 cm³ pasteurized milk

15 g sugar

1 egg

and a caramel topping prepared from 25 g sugar plus 2 tbsp. water.

Carefully record the preparation time and then bake in a cool oven at 175°C for approx. 40 mins. in small custard cups standing in a tray of water. Boil the milk and make up the packet mixes as recommended: also thaw out the frozen product. When all the crème caramels are cool assess them on the following basis:

(i) Price per portion (check the amount of milk used etc.)
(ii) Colour and appearance
(iii) Texture
(iv) Flavour
(v) Preparation time and cooking time
(vi) Storage requirements
(vii) Nutritional value

Work out from these results the best value for money.

What are the advantages and disadvantages of home made crème caramel? Would you consider that the packet mixes are an acceptable alternative?

2 A comparison of raspberry instant puddings available from different manufacturers

Make up a packet of Bird's Angel Delight with cold milk, carefully following the instructions on the packet and leave to set in several small dishes. Repeat this with several products marketed under 'own brand' labels again being careful to follow the instructions exactly. The products

A selection of raspberry-flavoured instant puddings (experiment 2) which can be ranked in order of preference using the Hedonic scale.

can then be compared in a variety of different ways.

a Assess each product as in experiment 1 on the basis of:
(i) Price per total packet and per suitable portion size including the cost of the milk.
(ii) Colour
(iii) Flavour
(iv) Texture
(v) Volumes obtained from equivalent quantity of milk
(vi) Preparation time

b *Order of preference.* Rank the different samples in order of preference or using the Hedonic scale described in Unit 22. If a large number of people can taste the samples then an overall class preference can be obtained.

c *Triangle test.* Find out whether the people tasting the foods can detect any difference between very similar products using the Triangle test. Three samples labelled ABC, (2 of which are identical) are arranged in a triangle and the tasters are asked to pick out the different one.

By these methods it should be possible to decide whether any of the 'own brand' products are identical to Bird's Angel Delight but marketed under the firm's 'own label'. Compare the ingredients of the different products to see if this is of any help.

From your results decide which of the products tested gives the best value for money.

What do you consider to be the nutritional value of these instant deserts in the diet, particularly when eaten by children?

Follow up

A similar type of assessment of instant desserts could be done on a variety of orange flavoured desserts; for example using the whip type products where milk is added, fruit fools with added fruit, mousses where only water is added and canned desserts, particularly looking at the cost and nutritional value as against acceptability.

25 Freezing I—browning of fruit

Aims

1 To investigate different methods for inhibiting the enzymic browning of apples.
2 To discover a suitable technique for avoiding the browning of apples when preserved by freezing.
3 To observe the changes taking place when a banana is frozen.

Introduction

Quick freezing is one of the safest and most efficient methods of food preservation. Provided that frozen food is stored at a low temperature — not higher than -18°C — nutritive value and quality are maintained; in addition less resistant micro organisms are destroyed while the growth of others is prevented. Although enzymes are not destroyed at -18°C their activity is greatly reduced.

Most food can be frozen without difficulty, but with fruit — particularly if it is light in colour — quality is lost due to *browning*. The browning of fruit is caused by the enzyme *polyphenol oxidase*. This enzyme acts on *tannins* present in fruit and in the presence of oxygen causes browning. Although browning is unsightly it is in no way harmful.

To prevent browning the following methods may be used;

a *Blanching.* Treatment with boiling water for a short time inactivates enzymes and prevents browning in most fruit (but bananas are an exception). Unfortunately blanching softens fruit and may produce a cooked flavour, though with fruit such as apples (particularly if they are to be used for cooking) the result may be quite acceptable.

b *Ascorbic acid.* Vitamin C prevents browning because it is a reducing agent and therefore reduces the tannins oxidised by enzyme action.

c *Acids.* Polyphenol oxidase works best at pH 4 and if the pH is reduced below this value by the addition of acid enzyme activity decreases.

d *Sugar syrup.* If fruit is immersed in syrup before freezing, air is excluded and as browning only occurs in the presence of oxygen it is prevented.

e *Sugar.* Fruit to be frozen can be packed in dry sugar. This slows down the action of enzymes and gives some protection from air.
As air is required for browning it is clearly important to exclude as much air as possible from the containers in which fruit is frozen.

Required

Equipment:
sharp vegetable knives (stainless steel)
small glass dishes e.g. petri dishes
1 large pan
stop clock
use of a freezer
bunsen burner or gas/electric ring
small freezer bags
freezer tape
plastic containers
aluminium foil

Materials:
2 kg firm cooking apples e.g. Bramleys
1 banana
sugar
commercial lemon juice e.g. PLJ
citric acid in a range of solutions e.g. approximately
    50 cm^3 each of 0.5%, 1%, 2%, 3%, 5% and 10%
ascorbic acid in a similar range of concentrations
sodium hydrogen sulphite in a similar range of concentrations
salt in a similar range of concentrations

Method

1 **Inhibition of enzymic browning of apples**
Firm unbruised apples of the same variety should be used for all the experiments, but only prepared immediately before they are required.
Peel, core and slice the apples thinly (approximately 25-30 slices per average cooking apple) using a stainless steel knife to prevent discolouration.
Treat the apple slices as instructed below leaving them in

Apples being prepared for freezing showing (from left to right) the effects of no blanching, under blanching, correct blanching and over blanching.

a glass dish. Observe any changes in colour and how soon this occurs and also whether there are any changes in texture after a period of at least two hours. If possible keep the slices overnight to observe any further changes. All samples should be clearly labelled and the results carefully recorded.

a *Control:* place 2 apple slices in a dry dish and leave exposed to the atmosphere.

b *Water:* cover 2 slices with cold tap water.

c *Blanching:* put 4 slices into boiling water and simmer for 15 seconds. Remove the slices and place 2 on a dry dish and cover 2 with cold water.
Repeat this process for different blanching times e.g. 30 and 40 seconds, 1, 1½, 2, 2½, 3, 4 and 5 minutes before removing from the boiling water.

d *Citric acid:* cover 2 apple slices with approximately 20 cm^3 of 0.5% citric acid. Repeat using higher concentrations e.g. 1, 2, 3, 5 and 10% citric acid.

e *Ascorbic acid:* repeat d using ascorbic acid solutions in same concentration range.

f *Sodium hydrogen sulphite:* repeat d replacing citric acid with similar concentrations of sodium hydrogen sulphite.

g *Salt:* repeat d replacing citric acid with similar concentrations of salt.

h *Commercial lemon juice:* cover 2 apple slices with approximately 20 cm^3 of 10% commercial lemon juice. Repeat with higher concentrations e.g. 15, 20, 25 and 50%.

How do these different treatments affect the browning?
Work out the optimum blanching times and solution concentrations required to inhibit browning without adversely affecting textures or flavour.
Find out the composition of the commercial lemon juice used including any preservatives added.
Which components of the lemon juice do you think are important in inhibiting the browning of the apple slices?

2 Freezing of apples

Prepare the apples in exactly the same way as for experiment 1 and treat in the different ways suggested below before putting in the freezer. If possible the apples should be left in the freezer at least a week, preferably much longer, before they are removed, allowed to thaw out and examined. Where the apple slices are soaked in a solution before freezing or packed dry they can be put in small 'freezer type' polythene bags and sealed with freezer tape. Where they are frozen in a solution, small plastic containers sealed with aluminium foil and freezer tape can be used. For these small scale experiments samples of approximately 10 apple slices should be used.

a *Untreated:* apples put straight into freezer bag.

b *Blanching:* blanch the apples for different times as in experiment 1 c and observe whether the slices go brown before or during freezing or on thawing. Notice any other changes in texture.

c *Salt:* using the optimum concentration of salt solution as found in experiment 1 g soak the apple slices in the solution for different lengths of time e.g. 5, 10 and 30 minutes before putting in the bags for freezing.

d *Commerical lemon juice:* repeat experiment c using the optimum concentration of lemon juice from 1 h and soaking the slices for different times. Also, using a similar range of concentrations as in 1 h freeze the apple slices in plastic containers with the lemon juice to see how this affects the browning.

e *Salt and sugar:* repeat experiment c using the salt solution and pack the slices in dry sugar after soaking in order to see whether this improves the colour, flavour or texture.

From the results obtained decide on the most suitable method for freezing apples in order to achieve the best colour, texture and flavour.

Follow up
In order to test the acceptability of the apple slices after freezing and to decide whether this is a worthwhile method of preserving them, various recipes could be made up comparing these samples with fresh apples particularly where the shape and texture is important.

3 Freezing of bananas

Take one whole under ripe banana and, without removing the peel, place it in a freezer for at least a week. Notice any changes in the appearance when the banana is first removed from the freezer and then allow it to thaw out gradually observing the changes that take place. When the banana is completely thawed, remove the peel and comment on the nature of the flesh.
Slices of raw banana could also be frozen in order to observe whether any changes which occur could be inhibited by salt, sugar, lemon juice or blanching as for apples.

Is freezing a suitable method of preserving bananas? Are the changes enzymic?

Quick-freezing of peas, showing them moving through a freezer tunnel on a cushion of cold air.

26 Freezing II–eggs and vegetables

Aims
1 To discover whether freezing is a suitable means of preserving eggs.
2 To find the optimum blanching time for freezing different vegetables.
3 To find a suitable way of freezing melon.

Introduction

Food is frozen in order to preserve it in a form in which the quality of the fresh food is retained. Food for freezing should therefore be frozen when it is in prime condition. For example, vegetables should be frozen while fresh, young and tender and fruit as soon as it is fully ripe. Most foods can be frozen successfully although some — such as leafy salad vegetables eaten raw — cannot, while a few — such as fruits with very high water content which are eaten raw(e.g. melons) — present problems.

Vegetables to be frozen usually require a preliminary *blanching* with boiling water in order to inactivate enzymes (see unit 25). Blanching preserves colour, flavour and nutritional value; without blanching vegetables soon produce unpleasant flavours. The blanching time varies with different vegetables — it needs to be long enough to inactivate enzymes but not long enough to cook the vegetable. After blanching, vegetables should be cooled as rapidly as possible.

When preparing vegetables for freezing all the pieces should be of approximately the same size e.g. sprouts should be graded so that all the sprouts in the same batch are roughly the same size. If this is not done neither the blanching nor the freezing will be even and there will be problems when cooking as not all the pieces will be cooked to the same extent.

Eggs can be frozen successfully but there are problems stemming from their nature. For instance, if eggs are frozen in their shells the egg white expands causing the shell to crack. The yolk of an egg is about one third fat, and this fat is in a highly emulsified form (see unit 27). When raw egg yolk is frozen the emulsion breaks down, water separates out leaving waxy lumps of solid that do not break down when the yolk is thawed. In order to freeze egg yolk successfully a stabiliser such as glycerine or sugar or salt (which lower freezing point) may be added to prevent emulsion breakdown.

Required

Equipment:
small pans
egg whisk/beater
basin
teaspoon
tablespoon
dropping pipette
stop clock
use of a freezer
bunsen burners or gas/electric rings
sharp vegetable knives
kitchen scales or balance
suitable freezing containers e.g. airtight cartons or foil dishes which can be sealed in freezer bags.
small freezer bags
freezer tape

Materials:
8 standard eggs
salt
sugar
glycerine
cream of tartar
cabbage
garden peas
cauliflower
sprouts
white turnip
1% solution of hydrogen peroxide
1% solution of Guiacol
1 large melon
1 small melon
lemon juice

Method

1 The freezing of eggs

a *Whole eggs.* Take 2 raw eggs and 2 hard boiled eggs and freeze them as indicated for at least a week before removing them from the freezer and observing any changes which have already taken place and those which occur when thawed:
  (i) raw egg, still in its shell
 (ii) raw egg, carefully cracked into an airtight container
(iii) hardboiled egg, still in its shell
(iv) hardboiled egg, with shell removed.

b *Egg whites.* Separate the whites from 4 raw eggs retaining the yolks for experiment **c** and freezing the raw whites as

Vegetables are blanched with boiling salted water and then cooled rapidly in cold water prior to freezing. What is the significance of the timer?

below removing them from the freezer for observation after a week:

(i) untreated
(ii) beaten to a stiff foam
(iii) beaten to a stiff foam with 1 tablespoon sugar
(iv) beaten to a stiff foam with pinch of cream of tartar

c *Egg yolks.* Freeze the 4 raw egg yolks in small containers, with the following additions, removing them for observation after a week:

(i) no addition
(ii) mixed with ½ tsp. salt
(iii) mixed with ½ tsp. sugar
(iv) mixed with a few drops glycerine.

What are the problems associated with freezing cooked eggs?
Make a list of the dishes containing hard boiled eggs which should not be put in a freezer.
What recommendations would you make as to the best way of freezing raw eggs:
(i) with yolk and white separated
(ii) with yolk and white together

2 The freezing of vegetables

a *Peroxidase test.* This simple test can be used to show whether the peroxidase enzyme which causes off flavours and colours in frozen vegetables is present in the food or if it has been inactivated by the blanching procedure. Place one drop of 1% *Guiacol* onto the cut surface of the vegetable followed by one drop of 1% *hydrogen peroxide.* The presence of a brown discolouration indicates that the enzyme peroxidase has not been inactivated.

b *Optimum blanching time.* Different vegetables are blanched in boiling salted water for increasing lengths of time and the peroxidase test is performed to see when the enzyme is inactivated.

(i) *Cauliflower.* Divide the cauliflower into small florets all of approximately the same size and wash well.
Use a small sample of the raw cauliflower for the peroxidase test before commencing blanching.
Boil 500 cm^3 of water containing 1 tsp. salt and blanch a 100 g sample of cauliflower in the water for ½ min.
Remove the cauliflower from the pan, immediately carry out the peroxidase test on a small sample and pack the rest into a suitable container along with some of the cooking liquid, ready for freezing.
Repeat this process for a blanching time of 1 min, and then also for 1½, 2, 2½, 3, 5 and 10 mins. using exactly the same weight of cauliflower in a fresh pan of salted water and performing the peroxidase test immediately after blanching.
After at least a week in the freezer, remove the samples, reheat and comment on their appearance, odour, flavour and texture.
Refer to the results obtained from the peroxidase test before deciding on the optimum blanching time for the cauliflower.

(ii) *Brussels sprouts.* Repeat experiment (i) using sprouts all

of which should be approximately the same size after preparation and washing.

(iii) *Cabbage.* Repeat experiment (i) using cabbage again prepared so that all the pieces are approximately the same size.

(iv) *Garden peas.* Repeat experiment (i) using freshly prepared peas.

(v) *White turnip.* Repeat experiment (i) using diced turnip.

Is there any difference in the optimum blanching times for these different vegetables? Can you explain these results?

3 The freezing of melon

The following experiments are designed to find the most suitable method for freezing.

a *Whole melon:* place a whole small melon in a freezer for at least a week before removing, thawing and observing any changes.

b *Melon slices:* divide a large melon in half, remove the seeds and place one slice about 2 cm thick in a suitable container for freezing.
Freeze for at least a week, thaw and observe any changes.

c *Melon cubes:* cut part of the remaining melon into 1 cm cubes and freeze a few of these cubes in freezer bags with the following additives.
Examine after 1 week.
(i) no further treatment
(ii) pack in dry sugar
(iii) soak in lemon juice and pack in dry sugar
(iv) soak in lemon juice and pack with a 30% sugar syrup.

d *Melon balls:* prepare melon balls from the remaining melon and treat in exactly the same way as for cubes.

Can you account for the changes taking place when a melon is frozen in the different ways suggested?
Which do you consider to be the best method of freezing melons?
If you can think of an improvement to this method, obatin some more melon and carry out further experiments.

Follow up

Various other types of food can be frozen quite successfully whereas some do cause problems. Using different samples observe the changes which take place when the following foods are frozen: red or green pepper, parsley, lettuce, bread, strawberries, milk and salad cream.
For each food decide:

a does it freeze successfully?

b are there any limitations to how the food can be used after freezing?

c could the product be improved by modifying the freezing procedure?

27 Colloids I–emulsions

Aims
1 To illustrate the two different types of food emulsions.
2 To investigate emulsion stability.
3 To find the best method for making mayonnaise.

Introduction
An emulsion is a mixture of oil and water, one of which is dispersed in the other in the form of very fine droplets. Such emulsions are of two types, either oil-in-water or water-in-oil. In the former small oil droplets (known as the *disperse* phase) are dispersed through the water (known as the *continuous* phase) whereas in the latter fine water droplets are dispersed through the oil. To identify the type of emulsion powdered dyes may be used. For example, if an oil soluble dye powder is added to a water-in-oil emulsion it will dissolve in the oil (continuous phase) and colour the emulsion surface. If a water soluble dye powder has been used it would not be taken up by the water (disperse phase) and the emulsion surface would not be coloured.

Oil and water are said to be *immiscible,* that is they will not mix. If they are shaken together vigorously they form a temporary emulsion which immediately breaks down. To form a stable emulsion a third substance called an *emulsifying agent* must be added. Egg yolk contains a good emulsifying agent and is therefore used in making salad cream and mayonnaise. Substances such as salt, sugar and spices also help to form a stable emulsion because of their capacity to 'hold' water. Synthetic emulsifying agents are also used, glyceryl monostearate (GMS) being the most common.

The texture of mayonnaise should be smooth and creamy and this depends on creating a stable emulsion containing extremely fine droplets. Such emulsions can only be achieved if the oil and water (in the form of vinegar) are mixed effectively and if sufficient emulsifying agent is present. With poor mixing or insufficient emulsifying agent the emulsion separates and is said to 'curdle'. Techniques that cause curdling are investigated in experiment 3 of this unit.

Required

Equipment:
test tube and racks
small glass dishes or tiles
mixing bowls
hand whisk
electric beater or blender
tablespoons, teaspoons
100 cm^3 measuring cylinder
10 cm^3 measuring cylinder
small containers for mayonnaise

Materials:
powder dyes — sudan III and methylene blue or similar
samples of:
   salad cream
   butter
   milk
   ice cream
   low calorie spread
1500 cm^3 cooking oil
400 cm^3 malt vinegar
12 eggs or 10 yolks and 2 eggs
salt
pepper
sugar
mustard
paprika
glyceryl monostearate (GMS)

Method
1 Identification of emulsions as water-in-oil or oil-in-water types
Prepare a mixture of 2 powdered dyes, one soluble only in oil such as sudan III, and the other a water soluble dye of a different colour such as methylene blue.
Sprinkle a *little* of the dye mixture onto the surface of the food on a glass dish, leave for a few minutes and then observe which dye has coloured the continuous phase. Use a wide variety of foods such as:- milk, butter, salad cream, ice cream and low calorie slimming spread in order to determine the nature of the emulsion.

What do you think happens when cream is churned into butter? (See unit 5).

2 Stabilisation of emulsions
Put 5 cm^3 malt vinegar into each of a series of 10 clean test tubes in a rack. Add the various ingredients as indicated below and shake 100 times. Observe the contents of the tubes immediately after shaking and also after they have been left for 10 minutes. Decide which tubes contain temporary emulsions and which permanent emulsions.

Additions:

a 5 cm^3 oil

b 10 cm^3 oil

c 15 cm^3 oil

d 15 cm^3 oil and 5 cm^3 prepared mustard

e 15 cm^3 oil, 5 cm^3 mustard and pinch of salt

f 15 cm^3 oil, 5 cm^3 mustard and pinch of pepper

g 15 cm^3 oil, 5 cm^3 mustard and pinch of sugar

h 15 cm^3 oil and 5 cm^3 egg yolk

i 15 cm^3 oil and 5 cm^3 egg white

j 15 cm^3 oil and pinch paprika

k 15 cm^3 oil and 1 g GMS

The conversion of cream into butter by churning involves the conversion of the oil-in-water cream emulsion into a water-in-oil emulsion.

Which of these substances exerts a stabilising influence on the emulsion?

Examine the ingredients of a French dressing and decide whether the emulsion will be temporary or permanent.

3 Preparation of mayonnaise

Basic recipe: 140 cm³ oil
30 cm³ malt vinegar
1 egg yolk
½ tsp. salt, ½ tsp. sugar
¼ tsp. mustard,   ⅛ tsp. pepper

Mix the egg yolk with sugar, salt, pepper and mustard. Add half the oil 1 tsp. at a time beating vigorously after each addition until the mixture is thick and creamy. Add 10 cm³ vinegar and then the remaining oil 1 tbsp. at a time still whisking all the time.
Stir in the remaining vinegar and leave the mayonnaise to settle in a separate container.

Modifications

a   control (using a hand whisk)

b   mix with an electric beater

c   add all the vinegar with the egg at the beginning

d   add the oil in 1 tbsp. lots at both stages

e   use 2 egg yolks instead of one

f   use only ½ egg yolk

g   use 1 whole egg instead of just the yolk

h   use 10 cm³ vinegar only, adding 4 cm³ initially

i   use 60 cm³ vinegar

Examine all the mayonnaises recording the degree of oil separation or curdling, their thickness, colour, flavour and general acceptability. Suggest an ideal recipe from your results.

What factors have caused the mayonnaise to curdle? How may this be (a) prevented (b) rectified once it has occurred?

Follow up
Find out the names of the emulsifying agents present in egg yolk and milk. In making commercial salad cream *stabilizers* may be added to increase the stability of the emulsion by increasing their viscosity. Edible starches and gums may be used for this purpose. Look at a number of commercial products and find out what stabilizers have been added.

During jam making lemon juice may be added to fruits which are low in acid in order to lower pH (top). As soon as jam is cool, jars should be well sealed (bottom); why is this? (see unit 28).

69

28 Colloids II–gel formation

Aims
1 To illustrate gel formation using pectin from different fruits.
2 To find the optimum conditions for the production of a pectin gel when making jam.
3 To investigate the problems associated with making pineapple jelly using gelatine.

Introduction
Certain substances, such as pectin and gelatine, consist of very large molecules which because of their thread-like shape are able to trap and immobilise relatively large amounts of water, so forming jelly-like solids known as *gels*. During gel formation the long molecules link loosely together to form a three dimensional network or mesh that gives the gel its stability. Gels, although solid, may be largely water and for example a gelatine gel may be 99% water.

When fruit is made into jelly or jam, pectin present in the fruit causes the jam to 'set' and form a gel. For satisfactory gel formation there must be the right combination of pectin, sugar and acid. Some fruit, such as apples and citrus fruit, are rich in both pectin and acid and can therefore be made into jam by adding sugar alone. Other fruit, such as peaches, are poor in both pectin and acid and in order to make satisfactory jam, sugar together with pectin and acid may need to be added to the fruit.

Where jam is made or stored with the wrong conditions various faults may occur. For example, if the pH is too low liquid oozes out of the jam and *syneresis* is said to occur. If water condenses on the surface of jam after it is bottled, sugar in the jam dissolves in the water producing an area of low sugar concentration that allows mould growth. If jam is boiled for too short a time too little *inversion* (the conversion of sucrose into *invert sugar*) occurs and this allows sucrose to crystallise so giving the jam a gritty texture. Overboiling on the other hand produces a weak gel and may cause invert sugar to crystallise.

Gelatine has remarkable setting properties which makes it easy to prepare gelatine fruit jellies. Pineapples do not form gelatine jellies readily because they contain the enzyme *bromelin* which breaks down gelatine thus destroying its setting properties. Pineapple jellies can nevertheless be made from cooked pineapple because bromelin is inactivated by heat.

Required

Equipment:
large and small pans
1000 cm^3 beakers
250 cm^3 beakers
100 cm^3 beakers
thermometers up to 115°C or sugar boiling thermometers
wooden spoons
sharp knives
bunsen burners and tripods or gas/electric rings
pH meter or indicator papers to cover range pH 2-4
muslin or cheese cloth
small round foil dishes or jelly moulds
scales or balance

Materials:
3 kg cooking apples
citrus fruit
fresh peaches or strawberries
sugar
citric acid
sodium citrate
pectin (150 grade)
gelatine
fresh pineapple
canned pineapple
tartaric acid
Fehlings solution I & II
methylated spirits

Method
1 Gel formation using pectin

a *Apples.* Cut a large cleaned apple into small pieces without removing the peel and boil in a small amount of water for approximately 20 minutes until it is soft and pulpy. Strain the mixture through a muslin cloth and retain the liquid in a weighed beaker. Measure the pH of the liquid using a pH meter or Universal Indicator solution or paper. Test for reducing sugars using Fehlings solutions I & II (see unit 5). Measure the pectin quality by taking a small amount of the liquid in a beaker, adding an equal volume of methylated spirits and shaking gently. Examine the clot or jellylike mass formed to see whether it is stiff or soft, all in one piece or in several smaller pieces. Calculate the weight of the remaining liquid and add an equal weight of sugar. Heat the mixture stirring until all the sugar has dissolved and then allow to boil for 10 minutes before leaving to cool and set. When completely cool examine the jelly produced.

b *Citrus fruits.* Use a large orange, two lemons or a grapefruit and after washing cut into small pieces again without removing the peel, pith or seeds. Boil in a small amount of water (approximately 100 cm^3) for at least an hour taking care not to let the mixture boil dry. Strain the mixture through muslin and measure the pH; test for reducing sugars and pectin quality as in experiment a. Boil the remaining liquid with an equal weight of sugar, and allow to cool as in a.

c *Peaches or strawberries.* Repeat a using suitable amounts (approximately 200 g) of either fresh peaches or strawberries cut up and boiled in a small amount of water.

Compare the strengths of the three jellies produced in (a), (b) and (c) and decide which is the most successful.

By looking at the pH, Fehlings and pectin clot results for each jelly, try and decide why some of these fruits form successful jellies whilst others do not.

What do you think are the critical factors in pectin gel formation?

2 The optimum conditions for the production of apple jam

a *Apple juice.* Wash 2 kg cooking apples and cut into small pieces without removing the skins or cores. Bring to the boil with 1000 cm^3 water and then simmer for 20 minutes until the apple is soft and pulpy. Strain through muslin and retain the liquid for the following experiments.

b *Apple jellies.* Prepare several samples of apple jelly according to the modifications below in order to find the optimum conditions.
Basic recipe: 50 g apple juice
                  50 g granulated sugar.

Boil the apple juice and sugar in a small pan stirring only until the sugar has dissolved. Continue boiling rapidly until the temperature is 105°C and then test a small portion of the liquid to see whether it will set by pouring it from a wooden spoon to a cold plate. When the test is positive pour the remaining jelly into small foil dishes and allow to cool and set. Store overnight, or even longer before examining the gels.

Modifications:
(i) *Effect of boiling temperature and time*
Prepare 4 jellies as in the basic recipe. Allow one sample to cool immediately after sugar has dissolved and boil the other samples until temperatures of 103°C, 105°C and 108°C are reached. Allow to cool.
(ii) *Effect of sugar*
Prepare 5 jellies as in the basic recipe but with varying amounts of sugar e.g. 20 g, 35 g, 50 g, 65 g, and 80 g boiling them all to 105°C before allowing to cool.
(iii) *Effect of pH*
Prepare 4 jellies as in the basic recipe but adjust the pH using citric acid to lower it and sodium citrate to raise it, to cover a range of pH values e.g. 2.5, 3.0, 3.5 and 4.0. Add 50 g sugar to them all and boil to 105°C.
(iv) *Effect of added pectin*
Prepare 2 jellies as in the basic recipe but add 0.1 g commercial pectin (150 grade) to one and 0.5 g to the other.

If possible leave all samples covered for a week and then examine them for the strength of the gel, crystallisation, syneresis or mould growth etc., before deciding which is the best sample. Also examine their flavour and mouth feel.

Why is it important to boil the jelly to a certain temperature? What effect will this have on the nature of the sugars present?
What is the effect of having (i) too much (ii) too little sugar in the recipe? Decide on the optimum value.
What is the ideal pH for the jelly to set? What happens at lower and higher pH's?

Compare the optimum jelly making conditions found in this experiment with the results obtained in experiment 1 and try to explain why the gels produced are of different qualities. Suggest a modification to the recipe for obtaining a strawberry jelly and explain how this could be used in the production of commercial strawberry jam.

3 Pineapple jelly
Prepare a number of samples of gelatine gels by dissolving 2 g gelatine in 10 cm^3 hot water in a 100 cm^3 beaker with the following additions. Leave to cool for approximately 1 hour before examining the jellies.

a control (no addition)

b 5 g crushed fresh pineapple

c 5 g crushed fresh pineapple after boiling for 10 minutes

d 5 g crushed canned pineapple

e 5 cm^3 canned pineapple juice

Examine the different jellies and compare their gel strengths, particularly noticing any differences between b and c.

Why do you think the canned pineapple behaves differently from fresh pineapple? What recommendations would you make as to the best way of making a well set pineapple jelly?

29 Organoleptic assessment I—taste thresholds

Aims

1 To investigate whether a person can differentiate between the four primary tastes.
2 To discover each person's threshold concentration for the four primary tastes.
3 To determine the threshold and optimum concentration of monosodium glutamate in a vegetable soup.

Introduction

The term *organoleptic assessment* simply means the use of our senses to evaluate food. We detect the flavour of food through the senses of taste and smell and in this unit we are concerned with the former.

The overall taste of food is made up of one or more *primary tastes* of which there are four, namely; sweet, sour, salt and bitter. The sensation of taste is detected by taste buds in the mouth, mostly on the upper surface of the tongue. Different parts of the tongue are particularly sensitive to different primary tastes. This is shown in the diagram in unit 30.

Our sensitivity to different primary tastes varies greatly. For example, we are so sensitive to bitterness that we can detect the bitterness of quinine at a dilution of 1 part of quinine in 2 million parts of water. On the other hand our sensitivity to sweetness is much less and we cannot detect the sweetness of a sugar solution until the concentration reaches 1 part sugar in 200 parts of water.

The lowest concentration at which a taste can be detected is known as its *threshold* concentration. We can distinguish two threshold values, one known as the *stimulation* threshold, when a tingling sensation on the tongue is an indication that 'something' is present other than water, even though the nature of the taste cannot be identified. The second value is the *identification* threshold which is the lowest concentration at which one of the primary tastes can be detected.

Monosodium glutamate. This substance is known as a *flavour enhancer* i.e. although it has only a faint taste of its own, it is able to enhance the flavour of many substances — particularly meat, fish and vegetable foods — to which it is added. It is now added commerically to a wide range of canned and dehydrated foods, usually in amounts of 0.1 to 0.3%.

Required

Equipment:
4 dozen small *clean* 100 cm³ beakers for tasting (or use clean plastic cups)
drinking straws
4 100 cm³ measuring cylinders fitted with stoppers
small pans or large beakers
vegetable knives
accurate electric balance
bunsen burners or gas/electric rings
1 very large pan

Materials:
100 cm³ of the following solutions:
2% sucrose
0.2% sodium chloride
0.05% citric acid monohydrate
0.05% caffeine
16% sucrose
2% sodium chloride
2% citric acid monohydrate
2% caffeine
salt, pepper
monosodium glutamate
carrots
onions
potato
peas
celery
stock cubes (which do not contain monosodium glutamate)
bayleaf or mixed herbs

Method

1 Recognition of primary tastes

Selecting sugar (for sweet), sodium chloride (for salt), citric acid (for sour) and quinine (for bitter) use the lower concentration solution for each of the four primary tastes (e.g. 2% sucrose not 16%) and also distilled water. Label 10 of the small beakers from 1 to 10 and transfer duplicate samples of about 50 cm³ of each of the above 4 solutions into 8 of the small beakers plus the water into the 2 remaining small beakers. This should be done in a random way so that only one person knows what is in each beaker. Each person in the group should taste the contents of the 10 beakers in turn using individual drinking straws. Do not swallow the solutions but let the liquid move over the whole area of the tongue and notice particularly where each different taste sensation is the strongest. Try to identify the contents of each beaker before moving on to the next one. Do not retaste any of the earlier beakers. When the tasting is complete, check the answers with the original coding and with the expected positions on the tongue.

Which of the four tastes do you find the easiest and the most difficult to identify? Can you give reasons for this?

2 Determination of threshold values

a *Preparation of solutions.* Use the higher concentration solutions of the four tastes for this experiment (e.g. 16% sucrose).
Take 4 sets of 12 beakers and label them A1 to 12, B1 to 12, C1 to 12 and D1 to 12.
Measure 50 cm³ of one of the solutions (e.g. sweet) into beaker A12. Make the remaining 50 cm³ solution up to

Students determining the threshold concentrations of the four primary tastes — sweet, sour, salt and bitter.

100 cm³ with distilled water in a measuring cylinder and shake well. Transfer 50 cm³ of this diluted solution i.e. half strength into beaker A11.

To the remaining 50 cm³ still remaining in the measuring cylinder add more distilled water to bring the volume back to 100 cm³, shake well and transfer 50 cm³ of this solution — now quarter strength — to beaker A10. Repeat this process of making up to 100 cm³, shaking and transferring 50 cm³ to the next beaker until all 12 beakers contain 50 cm³ of different strength solutions with beaker A1 being almost pure water. The final 50 cm³ left in the measuring cylinder can be discarded now to prevent confusion.

Repeat this process with one of the other solutions — e.g. salt in beakers B1 - 12 again starting with B12 as the most concentrated. The remaining solutions, e.g. sour and bitter are similarly diluted into beakers C1 - 12 and D1 - 12.

b *Tasting.* Each person should taste the four series of beakers commencing with beaker no. 1, then 2, 3, 4 etc., again using drinking straws and identifying the taste sensation on the surface of the tongue and mouth, without retasting any of the earlier solutions. On a piece of paper carefully record your reactions to each solution making particular note of which solution was identified as different from water and when the actual taste could be definitely identified.

Continue tasting, recording whether the taste is weak, medium or strong. When a solution becomes unpleasantly strong then tasting may stop even if beaker no. 12 has not been reached. Rinse the mouth out well with distilled water only when commencing a new series of 12 beakers. Stimulation and identification threshold values should now be available for all four of the primary tastes. The results of each member of the class should now be compared particularly noting the number of the beaker when the taste was first identified, in order to discover who has the most sensitive taste buds.

Is the same person always the first to identify each taste?

Question each member of the group as to the amount of sugar they have in tea/coffee — or who has a sweet tooth.

Does this have any bearing on the results for the sugar series?

Find out if any people have heavy colds and decide whether this has affected the results or not.

Do you expect heavy smoking to affect the results or not?

3 The use of monosodium glutamate as a flavour enhancer

Make up a large pan full of a basic vegetable soup recipe containing approx. the following:

250 g carrots
150 g onions
150 g potatoes
100 g peas
50 g celery
3 tsp. salt
pinch pepper
1 bay leaf or mixed herbs
2000 cm³ water
2 stock cubes.

Bring seasoned water plus stock cubes to boil and add finely chopped vegetables and peas to the pan. Simmer for about 1 hour. Carefully divide the soup into 10 equal batches in small pans. (alternatively prepare 10 samples from the beginning).

Keep one sample as a control with no further additives. To the other samples add increasing amounts of monosodium glutamate ranging from 0.25 g to approx. 5.0 g having rather more samples at the lower concentration levels. Simmer all the soups for a further 30 mins. until all the vegetables are fully cooked.

Taste all the soups commencing with the control sample and then those of lowest MSG level in order. Determine the identification threshold for the MSG and describe how it affects the flavour of the soup. Finally rank the soups in order of preference and compare your results with those of the rest of the class.

What do you consider to be the optimum level of monosodium glutamate in a vegetable soup? Do all those who tasted the soups agree with your recommended MSG level?

If not, find out from the class which people prefer packet soups to homemade or canned soups and decide whether this has any effect on their preferred levels.

Follow up

Visit a large supermarket and check the contents list of (a) soups (b) vegetable products and (c) meat products. Note which products contain MSG. In which of these types of products is MSG frequently used? What is the advantage to the manufacturer of adding MSG to such products?

30 Organoleptic assessment II–colour and flavour

Aim

To investigate whether the colour of food affects our sense of flavour.

Introduction

The colour of food is extremely important to our enjoyment of it. In unit 16 we noted the importance of the colour of fruit and vegetables and we investigated ways of cooking them that preserved an attractive colour. Most people are very sensitive to the colour of the food they eat and will reject food that is not considered to have the accepted colour. For example, strawberries that have been preserved in sulphite lose all their natural colour and appear white. If such strawberries are to be canned or used in jam, artificial food colour must be added before they are considered acceptable to eat.

Colouring matter is added to a large number of foods, particularly to convenience foods, to enhance its attractiveness. Some of these colours are natural in origin and have been used for hundreds of years. For example, the red colour of *cochineal* (obtained by crushing the bodies of dried insects) and the yellow colour of *saffron* (obtained from the saffron plant) have been familiar in food for many centuries.

On the other hand during the last hundred years many synthetic colours have been used in food. In Britain only those colours which appear in a permitted list may be used. It is important that any colour used in food should be clearly labelled as a 'food colour'.

There is a strong link between the colour and the flavour of food — and it is this link that is investigated in this unit. It seems that our ability to detect the flavour of food is very much connected with its colour and if the colour is unusual our sense of taste is confused! For example, if a fruit jelly is red it is likely that the flavour detected will be that of a red-coloured fruit such as raspberry or strawberry even if the true flavour is lemon or banana!

Testing a range of commercial soups to find out how their colour affects our sense of taste.

The depth of colour in food also affects our sense of taste. We associate strong colours with strong flavours. For example, if a series of jellies all contain the same amount of a given flavour, but are of different shades of the same colour, then those having a stronger colour will appear also to have a stronger flavour.

Required

Equipment:
12 small clean 100 cm³ beakers or cups
teaspoons
small pans or large beakers
wooden spoons
gas/electric rings or bunsen burners

Materials:
20 g gelatine
230 g sugar
30 g cornflour
1 pint of milk
salt
a wide variety of fruit flavoured essesnces
food colours

Method

1 The flavour of fruit jellies

Make up approximately 1 litre of unflavoured gelatine jelly using:
20 g dry gelatine (6 level tsp.)
200 g sugar
1000 cm³ water

Dissolve the gelatine in approx 200 cm³ of hot water and then add the sugar and the rest of the water.

Divide the solution between a number of small beakers and add a few drops of different food colours to each beaker. Using a wide variety of fruit flavours add a few drops of one of the flavours to each jelly so that there is not always the expected matching of colour and flavour; e.g. make up;

a a bright red banana flavoured jelly,

b a green raspberry flavoured jelly

c an orange blackcurrant flavoured jelly.

Stir well and allow the jellies to set. Label the jellies with a code number or letter and then allow several people, who are unaware of what flavours have been used, to taste them in turn and record what they think the flavour is. Check their results with the original coding to see if they are correct.

Has the colour of the jelly influenced the tasters in deciding what the flavour is or not? Can you explain this?

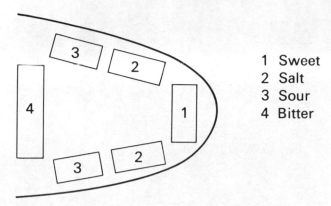

1 Sweet
2 Salt
3 Sour
4 Bitter

Taste sensitive areas of the tongue (see unit 29).

Are some flavours more easily identified than others? Can you suggest a reason?

2 The flavour of blancmange

Make up a basic cornflour sauce or blancmange using:
30 g cornflour
30 g sugar
568 cm^3 (1 pint) milk
pinch salt

Mix the cornflour and sugar to a paste with a small amount of cold milk and then mix this with the remaining milk which has been boiled. Stir well and bring back to the boil. Divide the hot sauce between several small beakers, and using the same basic flavour but in different known concentrations (e.g. 1 drop, 2 drops etc.) make up a series of 5 or 6 samples of the sauce.
Add the food dye so that each sample is a different colour or a different intensity of the same colour but not in the same order as the flavour concentration. Code the samples in a random way so that only one person knows which is which, and then allow several people to taste the sauces and then rank them in order of flavour concentration. Check the results with the original coding to see whether the taster has ranked them in the correct order.
It is suggested that one group uses different intensities of the same colour and another group uses a large range of colours. The results of the two groups can then be compared.

Have you been able to confuse your taster?
Is he/she most confused by the intensity of the colour or by the different colours?
From the results of this experiment is it true that we associate strong flavours with strong colours and vice-versa?

Follow up

Collect a number of convenience dessert products from a super-market e.g. a jelly, a blancmange and an instant whip. Make up the product as directed and ask a number of people who are blindfolded to identify the flavour of each. Check how many select the correct flavour. Remove the blindfolds, change the order of tasting (but do not tell the tasters) and allow the tasters to identify the flavour of the products that they now see. Check how many select the correct flavour. What difference does it make if the taster can see the product he tastes? Tell the tasters the correct flavours and ask their opinions as to whether they think the colour is appropriate for the particular flavour.

It has been said of convenience foods that the trend is towards flavours that are bland and colours that are weak. From your own experience do you consider this statement to be true or false? Give your reasons.

Reading suggestions

Although the introductions to each unit provide a brief theoretical background to the experiments, students will often want more information. The books given below will provide this.

Elementary Books

The Science of Food and Cooking, Allan Cameron, 1973, Edward Arnold. This book, which is designed for CSE and GCE 'O' level, gives an understanding of food and cooking at an elementary level and is intended as a companion volume to *Experimental Cooking.*

Food Science, G. Birch, M. Spencer and A. G. Cameron, 2nd ed., 1977, Pergamon Press. This book also covers the main topics required at an elementary level, but is particularly suitable for older students and adults.

Manual of Nutrition, eighth edition 1976, H.M.S.O. A brief booklet on nutrition, but valuable for its inclusion of food composition tables, required for example in units 5, 6 and 17.

More Advanced Books

The Experimental Study of Foods, Ruth Griswold, 1970, Constable. This is an extremely comprehensive book containing much detail and many references to original work. For students and teachers wanting to study topics in considerable depth this book will prove invaluable.

Food Science — a chemical approach, Brian Fox and Allan Cameron, 3rd ed., 1977, Hodder and Stoughton. This book covers the theory of most of the units and at a level that will be suitable for GCE 'A' level, for teachers in training and for students at Colleges or Further Education taking, for example, OND and HND courses in Catering subjects.

Food Science, Nuffield Advanced Science series, 1971, Penguin Books. Chapters 2 and 3 on food quality, food texture and changes in food will be useful particularly for those with an interest in chemical aspects.

Composition of Foods, R.A. McCance and E.M. Widdowson, revised ed., 1977, H.M.S.O. A standard and detailed compilation of the composition of foods (see particularly units 5 and 17).

Appendix 1–suppliers of special materials

1 Special chemicals

Chemicals that are not available in school or college, particularly the less common chemicals mentioned below, may be obtained from:

British Drug Houses Ltd.,
Poole,
Dorset, BH12 4NN

Name of chemical	Unit
Buffer tablets (or solutions)	2
Millons reagent	5, 7
Fehlings solutions I and II	5, 7, 20, 28
Tryspin	11
Papain	11
Glucono delta lactone	13
Calcium hydrogen phosphate (ACP)	13
Disodium dihydrogen pyrophosphate (ASP)	13
2:6 dichlorophenol indophenol	17, 23
Caffeine	29
Monosodium glutamate (order as ℓ - glutamic acid, sodium salt)	29
Guiacol	26
Glyceryl monostearate (GMS)	27

2 Special foods

Vegetable protein products required in units 21 and 22 may be obtained as follows:

(a)   Textured vegetable protein e.g. TVP from:
British Arkady Co. Ltd.,
Arkady Soya Mills,
Old Trafford,
Manchester M16 0NJ

(b)   Spun vegetable protein e.g. Kesp from:
Courtaulds Ltd.,
P.O. Box 16,
Protein Foods Unit,
Coventry CU6 5AE

Appendix 2 – table of metric and imperial units

Metric and Imperial Units

The following table shows how non-metric units may be converted into metric equivalents

	Non-metric	Metric equivalent
Energy	1 kilocalorie (Cal)	4200 joules (J) 4.2 kilojoules (kJ)
Temperature	32° Fahrenheit (F) 212° Fahrenheit (F)	0° Celsius (C) 100° Celsium (C)
	To convert °F into °C: -32° and then x 5/9	
Volume	1.8 pints	1 litre (l) 1000 cubic centimetres (cm^3)
	1 pint	568 cubic centimetres (cm^3)
	1 gallon	4.5 litres (l)
Weight	1 ounce (oz) 1 pound (lb) 2.2 pounds (lb)	28.4 grammes (g) 454 grammes (g) 1 kilogramme (kg)
Length	1 inch (in.) 1 foot (ft) 39.4 inches (in.)	2.5 centimetres (cm) 30.5 centimetres (cm) 100 centimetres (cm) 1 metre (m)

Practical Working Equivalents

The following equivalents, though not accurate, may be used for practical purposes:

	Non-metric	Metric equivalent
Volume	1 pint	500 cm^3
Weight	1 ounce	25 g

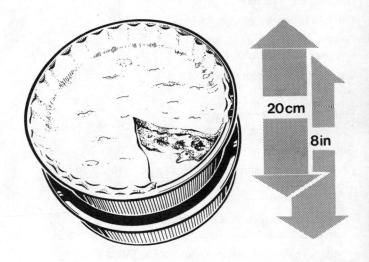

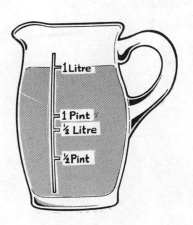

Acknowledgment

The publishers would like to thank the following for permission to reproduce copyright photographs:

Art-Wood Photography, courtesy of Philips 28; Bakery Information Service 35, 40, 51; Barnaby's Picture Library 5 (right), 11; Birds Eye Foods Ltd 65; Birmingham College of Food and Domestic Arts 73, 74; Ron Chapman 21; Colliers (Dover Street) Ltd, courtesy of British Egg Information Service 27; Courtaulds Ltd 59; Gene Cox Micro Colour (International) 14 (right); H J Green and Co Ltd 34; Grant Heilman 56; Anthony Kay, courtesy of Flour Advisory Bureau 39; Noeline Kelly 6, 7, 8, 10, 24, 26, 36, 43, 52, 63; Long Ashton Research Station 66; National Dairy Council 16; Popperfoto 25; Julie Stephens 44, 60, 69; Unigate 69 (top left); Vogue Studio 5 (left); Wheat Flour Institute 32; Wothington Foods Inc 57; Marilynn Zipes 14 (left), 20, 46.

STRANGE
Life Cycles

The Bizarre Life Cycle of a
KANGAROO

By Barbara M. Linde

Gareth Stevens
Publishing

Please visit our website, www.garethstevens.com. For a free color catalog of all our high-quality books, call toll free 1-800-542-2595 or fax 1-877-542-2596.

Library of Congress Cataloging-in-Publication Data

Linde, Barbara M.
The bizarre life cycle of a kangaroo / Barbara M. Linde.
    p. cm. — (Strange life cycles)
Includes index.
ISBN 978-1-4339-7048-1 (pbk.)
ISBN 978-1-4339-7049-8 (6-pack)
ISBN 978-1-4339-7047-4 (library binding)
1. Kangaroos—Life cycles—Juvenile literature. I. Title.
QL737.M35L56 2013
599.2'22—dc23

2012002832

First Edition

Published in 2013 by
Gareth Stevens Publishing
111 East 14th Street, Suite 349
New York, NY 10003

Copyright © 2013 Gareth Stevens Publishing

Designer: Andrea Davison-Bartolotta
Editor: Kristen Rajczak

Photo credits: Cover, p. 1 Jordan Tan/Shutterstock.com; p. 4 Eric Isselée/Shutterstock.com; p. 5 Rafeal Ramirez Lee/ Shutterstock.com; p. 7 Tom Brakefield/Stockbyte/Thinkstock; p. 8 idiz/Shutterstock.com; p. 9 Martin Harvey/Gallo Images/ Getty Images; pp. 10, 21 (top) Mark Newman/Photo Researchers/Getty Images; p. 11 © iStockphoto.com/4FR; p. 12 Serguei Levykin/Shutterstock.com; pp. 13, 21 (left) John Carnemolla/Shutterstock.com; p. 15 Ralph Loesche/Shutterstock.com; p. 17 Henk Bentlage/Shutterstock.com; p. 19 Anna Jurkovska/Shutterstock.com; p. 20 Inge Schepers/Shutterstock.com; p. 21 (right) timbles/Shutterstock.com; p. 21 (bottom) Meg Forbes/Shutterstock.com; p. 21 (center) Bojanovic/Shutterstock.com.

Printed in the United States of America

CPSIA compliance information: Batch #CS12GS: For further information contact Gareth Stevens, New York, New York at 1-800-542-2595.

Contents

Words in the glossary appear in **bold** type the first time they are used in the text.

Hopping Along!

Have you seen an animal that hops and looks like a large rabbit combined with a furry deer? It's a kangaroo! This **mammal** has soft fur, a small head, big lips, and large, rounded ears. It has sharp eyesight and hearing.

A kangaroo has two short forelegs (front legs) and two large, strong hind legs. Its long, powerful tail helps it balance and move. One of the most interesting things about a kangaroo is its unusual life cycle!

THE FACTS OF LIFE

Kangaroos belong to the Macropodidae (ma-kroh-PAH-dih-dye) family. This name comes from the Greek words meaning "long" and "foot."

4

Kangaroos are sometimes called 'roos.

A Unique Marsupial

A kangaroo is a kind of mammal called a marsupial. Marsupials are much like other mammals, but parts of their life cycle are quite different. A female marsupial has a pouch made of skin and fur on her stomach. Instead of growing inside their mother's body, baby marsupials, called joeys, do most of their growing inside this pouch.

Kangaroos have other unusual features, too. They can't walk on all four legs or move backwards easily. So, they hop to get around!

THE FACTS OF LIFE

A kangaroo can hop along at more than 30 miles (48 km) per hour, leap forward 26 feet (8 m), and jump 6 feet (1.8 m) high.

Kangaroos can't move their legs separately while on land. However, they can when they swim.

7

Finding a Mate

Kangaroos live in **mobs** made up of adult males, adult females, and joeys. The adult males often box with each other. The largest, strongest male wins and becomes the leader. Only this male will **mate** with the females. The leader spars, or fights, with the other males if they get too close to the females.

Some female mammals only have babies at certain times of the year. Not kangaroos! They can have babies at any time, although most babies are born in the summer.

kangaroo mob

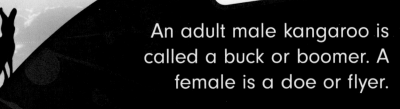

THE FACTS OF LIFE

An adult male kangaroo is called a buck or boomer. A female is a doe or flyer.

Kangaroo mobs may have
100 or more members.

A Baby Is Born

A mother kangaroo has just one baby at a time. It grows inside the mother for about 1 month, and then it's born. The **embryo** is about 1 inch (2.5 cm) long and weighs about 0.03 ounce (1 gram). It's so small that the mother can't even hold it.

The newborn is blind and doesn't have any fur. Its brain, heart, lungs, and other organs aren't fully **developed** yet. Its back legs aren't, either.

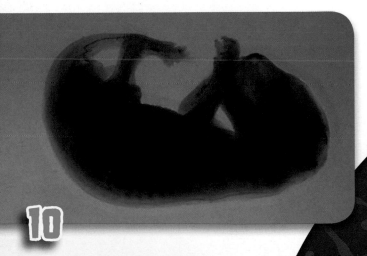

kangaroo
embryo

THE FACTS OF LIFE

A female kangaroo can start having babies when she's about 18 months old.

As the joey grows, parts of its body may stick out of the pouch.

A Cozy Pouch

The tiny embryo isn't ready to live in the outside world. It crawls up its mother's furry stomach into her pouch. Some scientists think it uses a strong sense of smell to find the way. The embryo uses its forelegs to climb.

The baby stays in the pouch, drinking milk its mother makes. Its fur and body parts grow. After about 7 to 9 months, the joey starts to come out of the pouch for short periods of time.

a joey in its mother's pouch

THE FACTS OF LIFE

The baby's journey up the mother's stomach to the pouch takes about 15 minutes.

A joey may jump into its mother's pouch headfirst if it gets scared!

13

A Joey-at-Foot

Out in the world, the joey begins to hop and eat grass. The watchful mother is only a few hops away. The joey returns to the pouch to sleep and drink milk. Other mothers and joeys are nearby. If people or other animals get too close, the mothers **defend** the joeys.

When the joey is around 11 months old, it leaves the pouch for good. But it stays close to its mother for about another year. Now it's called a joey-at-foot.

THE FACTS OF LIFE

Male joeys may play-fight, but usually the joeys in the mob don't play together.

Mother kangaroos talk to their joeys by making clicking noises.

More Babies

As soon as the joey is out of the pouch for good, the mother may have another baby. This newborn crawls into its mother's pouch to grow, even though the older joey still needs her. Her body makes a different type of milk for each joey!

A mother kangaroo only cares for two joeys at a time. However, she may have another embryo waiting inside her. It stays tiny until the baby in the pouch is old enough to leave.

A female kangaroo may stay close to her mother even after she has her own joeys.

The mother kangaroo stays close to the joey and keeps it safe from enemies.

17

Life with the Mob

The three most common **species** of kangaroos are the eastern gray, the western gray, and the red. They all live in Australia or on islands near Australia. They may live in small or large mobs, or sometimes alone.

Kangaroos are **herbivores**. They graze, or eat, the grass from fields or leaves from trees. The mob travels together to find food. Kangaroos eat in the cool mornings and evenings, and rest during the hot afternoons. They can go for months without water.

THE FACTS OF LIFE

Kangaroos can swim! They may swim across a stream to find food or escape an enemy.

These boxing kangaroos may be fighting over a mate or food, or just playing!

19

Kangaroo Cousins

There are many species in the kangaroo family. Tree kangaroos live in trees during the day. At night, they graze on the ground. Tree kangaroos sometimes look a lot like teddy bears! The smaller species within the kangaroo group are called wallabies. Rock and hare wallabies live in cracks in cliffs and under bushes.

These kangaroo cousins share the kangaroo's bizarre life cycle. But since no species is exactly the same, you should check out these amazing animals at your local zoo!

wallabies

The Life Cycle of a Kangaroo

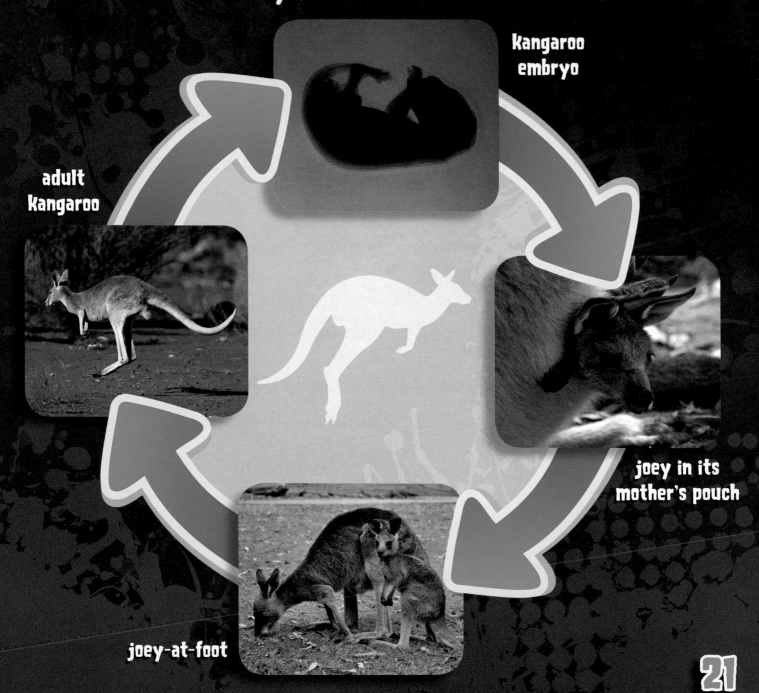

kangaroo embryo

adult kangaroo

joey in its mother's pouch

joey-at-foot

Glossary

defend: to guard from harm

develop: to grow and change

embryo: an animal in the early stages of growth, usually before it's born

herbivore: an animal that eats only plants

mammal: a warm-blooded animal that has a backbone and hair, breathes air, and feeds milk to its young

mate: to come together to make babies. Also, one of two animals that come together to make babies.

mob: a group of kangaroos that live together

species: a group of living things that are all of the same kind

For More Information

Books

Bishop, Nic. *Marsupials.* New York, NY: Scholastic Nonfiction, 2009.

Riggs, Kate. *Kangaroos.* Mankato, MN: Creative Education, 2012.

Websites

Kangaroos
kids.nationalgeographic.com/kids/animals/creaturefeature/kangaroos/
Learn more about kangaroos and see pictures of where they live.

Why do kangaroos hop?
animals.howstuffworks.com/mammals/kangaroo-hopping.htm
Find out more about how and why kangaroos move they way they do.

Index

Her baby rides on her back.

It holds tightly to her fur.

Mother and baby are looking for fruit to eat.

baby squirrel monkey

mother squirrel monkey

What is a squirrel monkey?

A squirrel monkey is a small **mammal** with a long tail.

An adult is only about 12 inches (30 cm) long.

However, its tail is 16 inches (41 cm) long!

Adult squirrel monkey size

tail

6

Squirrel monkey troops

Squirrel monkeys live in the rain forests of Central and South America.

They live in large groups called **troops** made up of more than 100 squirrel monkeys.

Each troop has babies, adult males, and adult females.

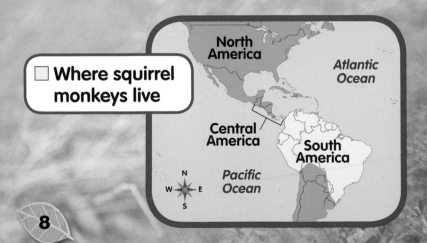

☐ **Where squirrel monkeys live**

North America

Atlantic Ocean

Central America

South America

Pacific Ocean

N
W E
S

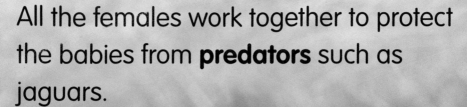

All the females work together to protect the babies from **predators** such as jaguars.

At home in the trees

Squirrel monkeys spend most of their time high in the trees.

They use their strong legs to jump from tree to tree.

Their long tails help them stay **balanced** on tree branches.

However, they can't hold on to the branches with their tails.

Baby squirrel monkeys

A mother squirrel monkey gives birth to just one baby at a time.

She keeps her newborn very close for the first few months of its life.

The baby rides from place to place on its mother's back.

baby sleeping

It is strong enough to hold on even as she leaps through the trees.

baby holding on to mother

Time to eat

Squirrel monkeys eat fruit, leaves, and small animals such as insects, lizards, and frogs.

They use their fingers to hold their food and to peel fruit.

A baby squirrel monkey learns how to find food by watching its mother.

When it is a few months old, the baby can find food all by itself.

14

squirrel monkey
eating fruit

Important sounds

Squirrel monkeys use more than 20 different sounds to talk to each other.

They shriek loudly to warn others when predators are nearby.

When they play, they make loud peeping noises.

A mother and her baby use sounds called chucks to talk to each other.

squirrel monkey
making a sound

Playing together

When a squirrel monkey is a year and a half old, it is a grown-up.

It leaves its mother and finds other squirrel monkeys to play with.

Together, the young monkeys find food and sleep at night in the trees.

All grown up

As adults, male and female squirrel monkeys stay with the same troop they grew up in.

For a while, the young females help care for other babies in the troop.

However, when they are three years old, females can begin families of their own.

Like their mothers, they will show their babies how to find food.

They will also teach them how to live safely in the tree tops.

adult squirrel
monkey

21

Glossary

balanced
(BAL-uhnst)
being upright
without falling

mammal
(MAM-uhl)
a warm-blooded
animal that has
hair and drinks its
mother's milk as
a baby

predators
(PRED-uh-turz)
animals that
hunt and eat
other animals

rain forest (RAYN FOR-ist)
a large, warm area of land
covered with trees and
plants, where lots of rain falls

troops (TROOPS)
groups of squirrel
monkeys

Index

Read more

Nickel, Bonnie. *Those Mischievous Monkeys (Those Amazing Animals)*. Sarasota, FL: Pineapple Press (2012).

Sjonger, Rebecca. *Monkeys and Other Primates (What Kind of Animal Is It?)*. New York: Crabtree Publishing (2006).

Windsor, Jo. *Squirrel Monkeys*. Boston: Houghton Mifflin Harcourt (2003).

Learn more online

To learn more about squirrel monkeys, visit
www.bearportpublishing.com/JungleBabies

About the author

Rachel Lynette has written more than 100 nonfiction books for children. She also creates resources for teachers. Rachel lives near Seattle, Washington. She enjoys biking, hiking, crocheting hats, and spending time with her family and friends.